Praise for 365 Bright Ideas to Market \

"If you are ambitious, this book will be a money machine for you. If you are unsure or overwhelmed, this book will be a lifesaver! "365 Bright Ideas to Market Your Indie Book," is the only step by step guide so flexible you can customize your approach and still get results by simply completing as little as just one of the book's tasks a day. Based on real-life time and budget considerations this book is made for you, and me, and every "authorpreneur" or publisher that wants to find their success. The author's wit and supportive style makes this not just a useful workbook, but also a feel-good book, too. That's why Happy Dolphin Press has adopted it as a part of our author tools for all of our publishing packages and a desktop essential for our team!"

—Jennifer Smith, *CEO Happy Dolphin Press*

"I know the author wrote this for indies but all authors would benefit from this book! I wish I had had it when my first book was released. I highly recommend it!"

—Angelina Assanti, *Bestselling Amazon author*

"As an award-winning author, I know first-hand that a best-selling book can sit in a box if the author does nothing to market his or her book. Patti Jefferson's "365 Bright Ideas to Market Your Indie Books" is a how-to guide about getting your book in the hands of readers. With witty practicality, Jefferson breaks down the marketing process with a combined recipe of advice and encouragement. This book is a must-read for all aspiring authors."

—Lisa Umina, *award-winning author of "Milo and the Green Wagon"*

"It states 365 but there are more than 1000 great ideas! This is a wonderful step-by-step guide for marketing!"

—LeeAnn Mancini, *award-winning Christian children's author*

"Many authors struggle because they love to write, but don't know how to market their books. *365 Bright Ideas to Market Your Indie Books* makes everything fun and simple for indie authors since it provides a roadmap you can follow (with entertainment breaks along the way), even if your time or money is limited. Your competition may tell you not to get any bright ideas, but I'm saying, "Get 365 Bright Ideas!" Your increased book sales will thank you."

-Tara R. Alemany, *founding partner, Emerald Lake Books and multi-award-winning author of The Plan that Launched a Thousand Books*

"Step by step, concise, easy to follow, this book is a "must have" for independent authors. Long overdue!"

—Kay Whitehouse – *multi-award-winning author of A Hand Truck Named Dolly*

"Patti Jefferson has put together what will certainly become a bible for authors. Whether you're a seasoned author or a novice writer, this workbook will ensure you leave nothing out when it's time to market your book. Full of step-by-step guidance, checklists, and examples, this is a must have on every author's desk."

—Timothy Jacobs, *Jacobs Writing Consultants, LLC*

"365 Bright Ideas to Market Your Indie Book is outstanding. Starting out in this industry can be overwhelming. There's so much to learn and an abundance of information to obtain. This workbook covers it all! There are step-by-step checklists, tips, templates, and URL data for all social media websites. This book not only helps new Indie authors but can help all authors and professionals in this industry. The compiled information in this workbook can be referenced for many years. A must have!"

—D.W. Harper – *Author, Illustrator and Publisher*

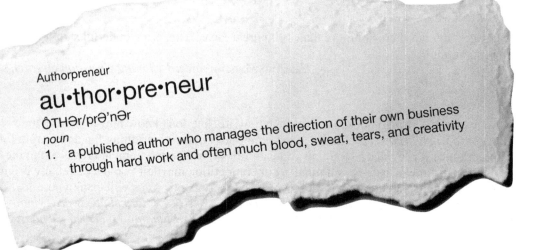

Authorpreneur

au·thor·pre·neur

ÔTHƏr/prƏ'nƏr

noun

1. a published author who manages the direction of their own business through hard work and often much blood, sweat, tears, and creativity

An Author's Practical Guide to Daily Marketing

365 bright ideas to market your indie books

(without a lot of money or time!)

A workbook by Patti Jefferson

Copyright © 2018 Patti Brassard Jefferson, PJ Inx Press

Library of Congress Control Number: 2018931863

ISBN 13: 978-0-9998404-0-5
ISBN 10: 0-9998404-0-1

COVER DESIGN:
Patti Brassard Jefferson (www.pbjauthor.com)
Light bulb design: BNP Design Studio thru Canva

AUTHOR PHOTO (Back Cover): Vandy Major for Florida Weekly
AUTHOR PHOTO (Page 27): Angel Dibbs Photography (www.angeldibbsphoto.com)

EDITORIAL SERVICES:
Jennifer Smith @ Happy Dolphin Press (www.happydolphinpress.com)

To all my Creative Weirdos, most of you know who you are.

....she shakes her head, muttering "authors" under her breath...

Preface

Over the past few years, I have had the privilege of working with hundreds of talented authors through my bookstore. I started writing this workbook after watching the constant struggle that some authors seem to have with marketing their work. As an indie author myself, I can attest that the struggle is real: it's not always a natural transition from author to marketer. This workbook is designed to make the bridge easier to cross so that authors can get back to doing what they do best... writing. It is my hope that participating in this workbook guides the reader into adopting the basic habits that authorpreneurs need to get their books out into the universe.

The challenge in creating this book is that the author spectrum is vast: from pre-production of the first book release to having multiple books in their catalog. So how to approach a workbook for those just getting started AND those who have been to this rodeo before? I have tried to include all of the important points that a novice needs to get on the right path. That part was easy because there is just so much to learn when you are starting out on this journey. My challenge was to fulfill the needs of the more advanced author. It became easier when I discovered that even those who have been in this industry for a while needed reminding of the basics and the ever-changing new options. Sometimes we forget the small things that build our foundation. This workbook will be your reminder.

On a personal note, I want to make clear that this book is not designed to be a gym membership that you start on Jan 1 and give up by Jan 25. Don't give up! If you miss a day, pick it back up. If you slack off for a week or even a month, forgive yourself and pick it back up. It's never too late to make marketing your book a habit. Complete the 365+ tasks. And then do it again. I'd offer you a prize for the accomplishment, but by then, you won't need it.

- pbj

Introduction

"The secret to getting ahead is getting started."
Mark Twain

We're in it together:

Most independent authors, no matter the genre, have a couple of things in common: their passion for their craft and minimal time/budget for marketing their published books. The classic vision of an author clicking around on their keyboard while wearing a sweater with suede elbow patches and casually sipping tea isn't very close to today's authors. Many have "regular day jobs" to go to, families to spend time with, and households to keep running. Where is an author supposed to find time to market their published titles and also find time to write the next chapter of the new book? In short, where are the magical marketing fairies?

Fairies disguised as a workbook:

Isn't that how it goes? You are fully prepared for the fairies to come take care of this whole marketing thing for you, and all you got was this dumb workbook. The truth is the fairies aren't coming and you will have to put in the time. Opera singer Beverly Sills once said, "There are no shortcuts to any place worth going." Marketing your book to more readers and getting your story into the hands of more people is the place worth going. This workbook is as close to a shortcut as you are liable to get.

Overview:

In this workbook, you will find 365+ tasks to market yourself and your book. Some tasks will only take a few minutes. Some will take much longer. The best part is, with the exception of the **First Things First** and **Author Branding** sections, tasks can be done in any order. The goal is to do at least one task every day until it becomes a habit to make time to market your book.

The Table of Contents:

Because this book can be used in a variety of ways, it has a unique layout. There are four ways to choose your daily task and two separate tables of content to facilitate your chosen method of usage:

- For the more traditional folks, who like to start at the beginning and work to the end, the pages are in numerical order in the Table of Contents on page 8.
- Authors with time constraints will find the Table of Contents by Time on page 10 to be helpful in figuring out what tasks should be done on busier days and which ones require more time to complete.
- For the budget-conscious authors, applicable costs have been added to the Table of Contents by Time.
- For the adventurous authors, just open the book and do whatever task is on that page!

The Key:

Each task will come with the icons you see in the box on the right: a clock to indicate how long the task should take, a piggy bank to let you know if there is a cost involved, and a calendar to indicate if the task should be repeated at certain intervals throughout the year. You can add those reoccurring tasks to the calendar in the back of the workbook so you can follow up on the appropriate day.

The Calendars:

The calendar pages in the back of the book were created blank so you can start at any year, month, or day and work daily for the next twelve months. Check the calendar before you begin a task each day to see if a reoccurring or follow-up task is already scheduled. Complete details on how to manage the calendars can be found in the **First Things First** section.

TASK KEY

The estimated time a task will take to execute.

The estimated cost a task will take to execute.

The number of times this task should be executed in the course of a year. Add these events to the calendar.

Table of Contents by Category

Check off tasks as they are completed.

Table of Contents by Time w/Costs

Check off tasks as they are completed.

- ☐ Your brand: Taglines ■ 24 ■ Free
- ☐ Goodreads author page ■ 37 ■ Free
- ☐ Street team ■ 45 ■ Free
- ☐ Media list ■ 52 ■ Free
- ☐ Press release ■ 53 ■ Free
- ☐ During and after event ■ 62 ■ Free
- ☐ Bookstore list ■ 72 ■ Free
- ☐ School list ■ 76 ■ Free
- ☐ HARO ■ 106 ■ Free
- ☐ Reading group guide ■ 116 ■ Free
- ☐ Social media networks ■ 139 ■ Free

1 HOUR+ TASKS

- ☐ Professional headshot ■ 26 ■ $75+
- ☐ Author website ■ 30 ■ 0-$20
- ☐ Website welcome video ■ 32 ■ 0-$50
- ☐ Author media kit ■ 38 ■ Free

- ☐ Event planning ■ 48 ■ Free
- ☐ Library sales ■ 94 ■ Free
- ☐ Book trailer promotion ■ 102 ■ Free
- ☐ Professional reviews ■ 110 ■ 0-$499
- ☐ Newsletters ■ 114 ■ Free
- ☐ Speaker packet ■ 132 ■ 0-$100
- ☐ Charity partnership ■ 142 ■ Free
- ☐ Schedule Facebook posts ■ 158 ■ Free
- ☐ Schedule social posts ■ 160 ■ Free

MULTI- PART TASKS

- ☐ Canva for DIY graphics ■ 18 ■ Free
- ☐ Pre-event promotion ■ 56 ■ Free
- ☐ The event bag ■ 60 ■ Free
- ☐ Book trailer planning ■ 100 ■ Free

First Things First

"The cost of being wrong is less than the cost of doing nothing."
Seth Godin

With a few exceptions, the tasks in this book can be done in any order. Those few exceptions have been placed under the **First Things First** and **Author Branding** categories.

In order to do any marketing for your book, the single most important task you need to accomplish is to clearly define your audience. Trust me when I tell you that "everyone" is not your target market. I promise. You can't figure out HOW to market your books if you don't know WHO you are trying to reach. The basic foundation of all your marketing efforts needs to be targeted and laser-focused in order to be successful. A scatter-shot approach will eventually give you at least some results, but a sniper approach will hit the target more often.

Other tasks that take place in the FTF category will lead you to:
• evaluate existing professional relationships
• figure out how to make your books stand out against the competition
• get organized to make the rest of the tasks in the workbook easier to manage

Let's get started…

Task: CALENDAR PAGES SET-UP
Category: First Things First

Unlike the gym membership tied to a New Year's resolution, this workbook is designed to start at any time, not just in January or always on a Monday. For that reason, the calendar is completely unformatted. Even the days of the week are left blank for the folks who like to start on a Monday and leave the weekend together at the end of the row and those who are more traditional and want a calendar that starts on Sunday. Set up your calendar however it makes the most sense to you. The important part is to GET STARTED!

Once you have added some of the recurring tasks later in the book, make it a habit to glance at the calendars before starting each day. You don't want to start a new task if something is already scheduled. When filling out the calendars with recurring tasks, pay close attention to what days of the week might be busier for you than others. If Tuesdays are full of soccer practice with the kids or Fridays are date night, don't add long tasks to those days. The recurring and follow-up dates are not rigid.

- TIP: You can also use the calendar to add dates of author events, workshops/ conferences, or book award deadlines. Adding these things will give you a blueprint for the next year as well.

- TIP: Add the page number of the original task so you can go back and use the information as a reference.

- TIP: When you finish a task, write it on the calendar for that day so you can see how much you have accomplished after a couple of weeks.

Sample:

Mon	Tues	Wed	Thurs	Friday	Sat	Sun
	1	2	3 Author event @ Bookstore	4	5	6 Preschedule social media (page 32) 1 hour

☐ **Wow! You are off to a good start! Add this completed task to today's calendar!**

14

Task: COMPETITION RESEARCH
Category: First Things First

Hopefully, before you hit the button to publish your book, you did a bit of research to see what titles and cover designs were like in your genre. Standing out in a crowded world is obviously your goal, but identifying existing trends will help you hit the mark when introducing a new product to the market. Tweaking, instead of reinventing, the wheel is both smart and time/money-saving.

Once you have identified the best-sellers in your genre, follow them on social media so you can make note of what they do since their audience is likely the same as yours. Use their expertise as inspiration to step up your game. After all, they are the people who are where you want to be.

How-to Steps:

One of the easiest ways to see who the best-selling authors are in your genre is to go to: https://www.amazon.com/best-sellers-books-Amazon/zgbs/books. Amazon updates these lists hourly, but realize some may be classics and duplicating their marketing efforts would be impossible (I don't think Mark Twain is on Twitter). With a list of 100, you should be able to find at least a handful of authors to keep an eye on.

TIP: Choose independently published books where the authors themselves or a small team is doing the bulk of the promotion.

1. Author: _____
   Website:_____ Social Media:_____

2. Author: _____
   Website:_____ Social Media:_____

3. Author: _____
   Website:_____ Social Media:_____

4. Author: _____
   Website:_____ Social Media:_____

5. Author: _____
   Website:_____ Social Media:_____

☐ **Another one done! Add this completed task to today's calendar!**

Task: YOUR AUDIENCE DEFINED

Category: First Things First

Before you can make any sort of marketing plan, you have to define your audience. It's easy for an author to say, "My target market is *all* readers." This statement isn't even remotely true! Defining your market will make it easier for you to do targeted marketing and make better decisions on where and how you spend money and time.

The Checklist:

Take some time to honestly answer these questions about your audience. Ideally you figured this out prior to writing the book, but revisiting the information now will let you create more targeted marketing. Remember, your *reading* audience is not necessarily your *buying* audience, especially in the children's book genre. Of course, you can have more than one target market but focus on just one for now. In a few months, redo the exercise to expand your audience.

Not sure how to find info on your audience?

- TIP: If you already have a book published, collect info from your existing audience.
- TIP: Use social media or email to conduct a survey, reader interviews, or focus groups.
- TIP: Use Facebook or Twitter algorithms to narrow down information about your existing audience.
- TIP: Research publications/newsletters and groups/organizations your readers are most likely to subscribe to or join. Use their demographics to help create your own.

Reader Info:

1. What is your hook? (ie. what is unique or special about your book?)

   _____

   _____

2. Buyer age range: _____ Reader age range: _____

3. Gender: _____

4. Education level: _____

5. Income: _____

6. Occupation: _____ Retired? _____

7. Married / Single / Divorced / Widowed: _____

8. Do they have children? _____ Parents? _____

9. Ethnicity: _____

10. Religion: _____

11. Country / region / language / climate: _____

12. Social class: _____

13. Special features: _____

14. Social media platforms they use:

    _____

    _____

Using the information you have gathered, write a profile for your perfect book buyer to connect with your characters and story. You can even give them a name!

_____

_____

_____

_____

_____

_____

Now that you know WHO they are, we can explore WHERE they are!

☐ **You are on a roll! Add this completed task to today's calendar!**
☐ **Add to Calendar:** *6 months from today*

17

Task: CANVA FOR DIY GRAPHICS

Category: First Things First

In a perfect world, an author would pay for professional designers to create all of the graphics needed to market their books. In reality, however, more and more authors are taking charge of their own graphics. Using a simple program such as Canva can make your marketing get noticed and look more professional.

Canva is a free graphic design program that can be used by novice designers and seasoned professionals alike. It has a user-friendly drag-and-drop interface and access to millions of photos and illustrations — many free of charge. One of the best features is all of the various sizes for social media or print materials available as templates so there is no second-guessing what will fit where!

How-to Steps:

1. Sign up for your free account. There is a category called *Writer/Author* which will narrow down the 50,000 templates for you.
2. Go to https://designschool.canva.com/tutorials/ and walk yourself through the hands-on tutorials. They will take from 5 - 10 minutes each on average, depending on your level of prior design knowledge.
3. Check off each section upon completion and make notes for yourself:

Getting Started
☐ Beginners' Challenge _____
☐ Essential Canva Tools _____
☐ Less is More _____

Fonts
☐ Choosing the Right Font _____
☐ Font Pairing Basics _____
☐ Tips for Titles _____

Color
☐ Choosing the Right Font _____
☐ Font Pairing Basics _____
☐ Tips for Titles _____

Images
☐ Using Canva Grids _____
☐ Enhancing Images _____
☐ Fantastic Photo Filters _____

Backgrounds
☐ Marrying Text and Images _____
☐ Brilliant Backgrounds _____
☐ Creative Background Tools _____

Shapes and Icons
☐ Designing with Shapes _____
☐ Introduction to Infographics _____
☐ Starting with Scale _____

Layout
☐ The Art of Alignment _____
☐ Working with White Space _____
☐ Harnessing Hierarchy _____

Branding
☐ Building a Brand Kit _____
☐ Consistent Branding _____
☐ Designing a Presentation _____

Advanced tips
☐ Canva Shortcuts Part 1 _____
☐ Canva Shortcuts Part 2 _____
☐ Canva Tips and Tricks _____

Skills in Action
☐ Design for Social Media _____
☐ Perfect Presentations _____
☐ Tweak Those Designs _____

Notes: _____

_____

_____

TIP: When downloading graphics that have a price attached, make sure you choose the correct licensing agreement to avoid any conflict down the road.

TIP: Premium graphics may cost $1 extra upon download. You can buy them at a discount if pre-purchased in bulk numbers — without upgrading your account.

TIP: Upgrading to a **Canva for Work** account will allow you to upload your own fonts and brand colors, organize with folders, access over 300K graphic images, and resize your designs to fit other templates. It may be well worth the expense if you are using Canva frequently to create your marketing materials or social media posts.

☐ **Well, la-te-da! Add this completed task to today's calendar!**

Author Branding

**"Products are produced in the factory, but brands
are produced in the minds of the consumer."**
Walter Landor

The most successful companies in the world market have recognizable attributes such as logos, colors, slogans, and presentation. Think McDonald's... do you know what their logo is? And what colors the employees' uniforms are? Their store layouts, their mobile app, and marketing campaigns are all consistent with their brand of a family friendly and fun place to eat. The fast-food giant has been around since the 1950s and while their brand has evolved with changing times and trends, it has also stayed remarkably identifiable.

Your author brand is more than what colors you use in your logo or what your website looks like, although those are obviously important as part of a much larger package. A purposeful author brand allows you to combine all of the things that represent you and your business for a common goal. Creating a consistent voice, style, and look will allow your readers to not only identify your work more easily but build your reputation as a professional and an expert.

While there are many small elements that will make up your author brand, the key is to be consistent in your execution. Spending time now to deliberately plan your brand may make all the difference in your success.

Task: YOUR BRAND: LOGO
Category: Author Branding

A logo is defined as a graphic representation of your company and its products. It is important to remember that a logo is NOT your brand but rather an element of your brand. Your brand is your overall corporate image. Elements of a good logo include: simplicity, relativity, potential longevity, size and media adaptability, and memorability.

The Checklist:
Do you have a logo?

☐ Yes! Four adjectives I think my logo says about me:

1. _____
2. _____
3. _____
4. _____

☐ No, not really. I should work with a graphic designer to come up with one. Four adjectives I want my logo to say about me:

1. _____
2. _____
3. _____
4. _____

💡 TIP: Your logo can be as simple as your signature or a complex, more detailed design. Hire a professional if this is outside of your expertise. Your logo is too important to leave to amateurs.

💡 TIP: Choose a font (letter style) and a couple of colors you can consistently use in your marketing including book covers, social media, website, etc.

💡 TIP: Make sure you know what your hex codes are for the colors you use if you are creating your own graphics. Don't just pick your favorite colors, research to see what emotions each color invokes. Consider genre and message when choosing colors.

💡 TIP: A couple of good resources for fonts to use in your logo are: www.fontsquirrel.com, www.dafont.com, and www.fontspace.com. Remember to use decorative fonts sparingly and NEVER use all caps with a scripted font. EVER!

☐ **Victory! Add this completed task to today's calendar!**

Task: YOUR BRAND: OTHER ELEMENTS

Category: Author Branding

Brand elements other than logo may include patterns, backgrounds, icons or symbols, or any other graphic add-on. Brand elements can also be a "feel" or attitude. For example, Jane Wood (www.janewoodbooks.com) writes mystery and adventure books for middle-grade readers. Her book covers include maps of the locations used in her books. Her website also has a compass theme. These would be branding elements that are not her logo. Her consistency in using these sorts of elements gives the reader a sense of what her books are about without even reading her blurbs!

The Checklist:

Do you have any other brand elements?

☐ Yes! These:

_____

_____

_____

☐ Not really. Here are some things I might consider:

_____

_____

TIP: If you do have specific brand elements, be consistent in their use throughout your marketing materials, website, and social platforms.

Do your website, blog and social platforms have a cohesive look? While each social platform has its own target audience and its own voice, keeping your author brand the same across platforms is an important way to create strength in your brand.

☐ Yes! I use the same:
    ☐ color palette
    ☐ brand elements
    ☐ tagline

☐ No, I have no cohesion yet. Here are some things I might consider:

_____

_____

TIP: Use similar headers on your social media platforms. The pro version of Canva lets you use one design in a variety of different sizes.

☐ **Impressive! Add this completed task to today's calendar!**

Task: YOUR BRAND: TAGLINES
Category: Author Branding

A tagline is also sometimes called a slogan or a catchphrase and is a staple in marketing and advertising of many famous products and brands.
See if you can remember any of these:

Bounty (paper towels) : _____

M & M's: _____

Nike: _____

Answers to tagline above: The Quicker Picker Upper, Melts in your mouth, not in your hands, and Just do it!

The purpose of the tagline is to make a product memorable to the audience. An author's tagline is like the subtitle to a book. It gives the reader an idea of what you, as an author, or your books, as a whole, are about. It should inform first and foremost but may also have other attributes:

- Establish you as an "expert in your field" such as *PJ Boox - The Indie Authors' Indie Bookstore.*
- Create a concise mission statement or description of your body of work such as *Happy Dolphin Press - We Take Fun Seriously.*
- Play on your name or the name of your book/series such as my *"Kids love PBJ!"* (a play on my initials).
- Address your genre such as Jane R. Wood's tagline, *"Mystery and Adventure Make Reading Fun For Kids."*

The Checklist:

Do you have a tagline?

☐ Yes! This:_____

And I have added it to:

      ☐ my website

      ☐ my blog

      ☐ Facebook and other social media platforms

      ☐ my electronic media kit

      ☐ my print material

☐ No. I don't have a tagline YET!

    💡 TIP: Read the reviews and comments from your readers to see if there are any recurring phrases. That just might be your tagline!

    💡 TIP: Keep it short!

☐ **You've got this! Add this completed task to today's calendar!**

Task: AUTHOR BIO

Category: Author Branding

There are many places you will need to use an author bio, yet many authors struggle with what to say about themselves. Fine-tuning your bio is important as it will be needed for your books, your website, social media, media kits, blog, interviews and more. You don't want it to be too long or too short, and you definitely don't want it to come across as boring. Your bio is how potential readers will initially connect with you. That connection could have a significant impact on your book sales.

Depending on your genre, you'll need a couple of different versions of your bio:
- Serious and detailed (the back of your book or press releases)
- Light and entertaining (social media bios often fall in this category)
- Short and sweet (you aren't telling your whole life story)

For reference, versions of my bio can be found on the back of this book, previous books, my website, and all of my social media platforms.

The Checklist:

The only hard and fast rules about writing your author bio are that you maintain your voice, remember your audience, and keep it up to date. Here are a few other things you may wish to consider when you write/rewrite your bio:

☐ Write in the third person. This is a professional bio, not an autobiography. You are establishing yourself as a credible professional.

☐ Determine if it is important to include credentials such as memberships to professional organizations, advanced education achievements or job titles, and experience in a related field. No need to talk about your degree in architecture if you have written a children's book about puppies. However, do include it if your book is about the history of old buildings in New York City.

☐ Mention literary awards if applicable. Keep in mind most people may not be familiar with specific awards so if they are numerous, consider saying something like, "John Smith has won over twenty awards for his books, including the prestigious *Best Book in the World* award."

☐ Is a call to action (CTA) appropriate? Possible CTAs might be "You can follow John on Facebook and Twitter" or "Learn more about Mary on her blog, *One Crayon Short.*"

☐ Delete anything that isn't interesting or necessary.

☐ **I have faith in you! Add this completed task to today's calendar!**
☐ **Add to Calendar:** *6 months from today*

Task: PROFESSIONAL HEADSHOT

Category: Author Branding

A professional headshot is literally the face most of your readers will put with your work. It is acceptable to have more than the one headshot used on the back of your books or on social media or print material but, again, the look and feel of them should be consistent.

> TIP: Think the photo you are currently using stacks up? Do a Google image search for "author headshot" and compare. If you think you might need to step up your game, continue with this task....

How to Find A Photographer:

There isn't really one main source to find photographers, but most working professionals will have a web presence on all major social media platforms, as well as their own websites.

> TIP: Start by using keyword searches like: <professional headshots>, <personal branding photography>, <business and corporate headshots>, or <headshots for creative professionals>.

> TIP: Google will usually list local pros first, but if you're looking for a particular location, be sure to name the city in your search.

> TIP: LinkedIn is a great tool for industry-specific database searches, but Google will be better at narrowing down zip codes/cities.

> TIP: Ask other business professionals in your circle to recommend someone and take a look at examples. Real estate professionals, legal professionals, and other authors may have recommendations. Remember, you are looking for good professional headshots, not graduation, wedding, or pet photographers. Hire a specialist.

Photographer: _____

Phone/Email: _____

Recommended by: _____ Price range: _____

******

Photographer: _____

Phone/Email: _____

Recommended by: _____ Price range: _____

******

Photographer: _____

Phone/Email: _____

Recommended by: _____ Price range: _____

Tips for a Successful Photo Shoot

- ⚲ TIP: Remember your branding! Use color schemes that complement your logo and other elements. Find locations that reflect your brand or genre.
- ⚲ TIP: Make sure your clothing reflects your voice/genre. Choose different accessories or clothing layers to get different looks.
- ⚲ TIP: If you know a representative from a beauty company (Mary Kay, Avon, etc.), ask them to do your makeup or give you advice. They are usually happy to help in exchange for before and after photos. (Buy some product to show your support, especially if they help you at no cost!)
- ⚲ TIP: Don't wear clothes with busy patterns or use cluttered backgrounds.

Still thinking it doesn't make a difference if you skip using a professional photographer? Check out my first headshot taken with a phone in my yard and then the other two taken by professionals. Yeah... it's like that.

☐ **Looking good! Add this completed task to today's calendar!**

Task: AUTHOR DOMAIN AND EMAIL

Category: Author Branding

A website is a must-have marketing tool for authors and, while that can mean different things to different people, the domain name is the first step. If you already have a domain name, read through this task anyway so you can make sure you are already making the best decisions about your domain and you haven't missed something.

If you don't have a website yet, or don't plan to create one, buying the domain name still might make sense for no other reason than to keep others from buying it and confusing people who are looking specifically for you.

Your domain name or URL (Uniform Resource Locator) is the "address" your website uses on the World Wide Web. Deciding on a domain name is important to your author brand as it will be used in all of your marketing and contact information.

Things to consider when choosing a domain name:

1. Keep it short and simple! Mine is pbjauthor.com because Patti Brassard Jefferson is a long name and not easy for everyone to spell.
2. Use something that will be relevant as your business grows. If your domain name is the title of your book, what happens when you write the second one? If you choose something kid-relevant because you publish children's books, what happens if you decide to add a YA title?
3. Does it fit in with your other social media platform brands?
4. Avoid unnecessary numbers, symbols, or spellings. The more you have to explain your domain name, the less effective and memorable it is.
5. Pick the best suffix for your URL: .com is still the most preferred, but you can often buy additional suffixes for reduced pricing to keep others from buying domains similar to yours and causing confusion.

The Checklist:

☐ I already have a domain name: _____

☐ I have a website, but it is www.myname.websitebuildingcompanyname.com and has hosting advertising on the pages.

   💡 TIP: This is a sign of a free website and is generally regarded as less professional. It's time to upgrade!

☐ I do not yet have my own domain name but will by the end of this task!

   💡 TIP: Tell 10 people your potential domain name and ask them to spell it. If more than a few people struggle to spell it, then you need to simplify it.

   💡 TIP: Write out your domain name to make sure it doesn't spell an unfortunate or offensive word when put together. (Go to boredpanda.com/worst-domain-names for some interesting examples!)

    TIP: Don't buy your URL until you have checked that the same name is available on all of your social platforms as well. You will want to be consistent! Don't be *joeauthor.com* on your website, *@joesbooks* on Twitter, and *facebook.com/joewritesbooks1234*. Make it easy for fans to find you!

How-to Steps:

1. Select a domain name REGISTRAR. There are many different companies with the most popular being: GoDaddy, Namecheap, and Domain.com. These companies are often running specials on pricing but be sure to read the fine print for add-ons and extended durations.

       TIP: You will also need to find a HOST for your website. Many hosts will provide a free URL with their packages which will still be dictated by availability. Make sure you read the fine print to ensure you will retain all rights to your domain name.

   Note: I use GoDaddy as my registrar and Wix as my host as I find it more user-friendly and easy to do on my own.

2. You may select your email address when you order your domain name. Some registrars offer an email address free with your domain. *Note: GoDaddy charges a very small monthly fee.*

       TIP: Remember your author branding and pick an email address consistent with your brand. For instance, info@mydomain.com or yourname@yourdomain.com are good examples of strong email addresses.

3. You should also set up a Google email account as well if you don't already have one. You will need this to set up a Google+ page or a YouTube channel even if you don't use it to receive emails. (Instructions for setting up a gmail account can be found at https://accounts.google.com/SignUp)

       TIP: If you are already using Gmail anyway, you can set up email forwarding so emails going to yourname@yourdomain.com actually end up at yourdomain@gmail.com. (Instructions for setting up forwarding can be found at https://support.google.com/mail/answer/10957)

       TIP: Remember to change your *send mail as* settings to your new non-Gmail address so people who get emails from you won't be confused.

☐ **You did it! Add this completed task to today's calendar!**

Task: AUTHOR WEBSITE

Category: Author Branding

Many authors feel that in this day and age of social media, they don't need to have an author website anymore. That's simply false! Studies have shown a large number of readers get information about individual authors through their websites. Think about it... it's the one place the author gets to call all of the shots — no social media restrictions on design, content, or engagement! When a potential reader searches the internet for you and finds your website rather than just your listing in an online book catalog, you have their undivided attention.

If you already have an author website, kudos! Skip the "How- to Steps" instructions. Walk through the checklist to make sure you haven't forgotten anything and your information is current.

For a more in-depth look at authors and websites: http://dgregscott.com/your-internet-identity/

How-to Steps:

1. Use your author branding elements (color, logo, etc.) to design your website. Some information you may want to include:

    ☐ Home page

    ☐ About the Author page with author headshot and bio

    ☐ Shopping cart if you plan to handle your own sales

    ☐ Links to websites where your books can be purchased if you do not plan to handle your own sales.

    > TIP: Don't just link online sources. Add links to any retail locations that may also carry your books.

    ☐ An email capture form (for example: "Subscribe to my newsletter," "Add your email to get updates on new releases," "Register to win a free ebook")

    ☐ Contact info: your email, blog, and social media links. Make it easy for them to find you!

    > TIP: Use live links people can click on to direct them to your social media platforms.

    > TIP: If possible, use a form to accept emails to avoid spam from posting your actual email address.

    ☐ Blog (if you have one)

    ☐ Author Events Calendar

    ☐ FAQ

    ☐ Media Kit

2. Get recommendations from other authors for reliable, easy to use website builders. By going through this task page so far, you will have a clear idea of what you want or need in a website and will be able to communicate with your webmaster.

3. If you opt to go the DIY route, research a few different website development platforms. Luckily, there are a lot of options out there for various levels of technical competency. The chart below has some of the more popular site builders as well as features and pricing. Note: All of the platforms listed have free custom domains and mobile app capabilities. Do your research and give each one a test drive to see which one is right for you.

4. All of these website builders have extensive videos, FAQ and other tutorials to guide you through the process of actually setting up your website. They also all have great support staff who will help you get through any challenges.

Platform	Cost/month	Free option	E-com or storefront	Email	Ease of use
Wix	$5 - 25	Yes	Yes	No	5/5
Square	$12 - 40	14d trial	Yes	Yes	4/5
Weebly	$8 - 38	Yes	Yes	No	5/5
GoDaddy	$6 - 15	No	Yes	Upgrade	4/5

5. Whichever platform you use, there will be step-by-step instructions on how to connect your new site to your personalized domain name.
   - TIP: It's okay to use the free version while you get everything set up but once the website goes live, upgrade to a level that lets you use your own domain name. There will be advertising for the website company on the free version, and you will end up with a domain name that screams "unprofessional!"

6. Select a few people to proofread your website and test any live links.

7. Promote your new (or updated) website on your social media platforms and to your email list.

☐ **Keep it up! Add this completed task to today's calendar!**
☐ **Add to Calendar:** *Update your information* **3 / 6 / 9** *months from today*

Task: WEBSITE WELCOME VIDEO

Category: Author Branding

Five startling statistics about video use in marketing:
1. 55% of people watch videos online every day.
2. Just using the word video in an email post increases the open rate about 19%.
3. 500 million people watch videos on Facebook every day.
4. Marketers who use video on their websites and other social platforms grow their revenue 49% faster than those who do not.
5. Over 50% of marketers across the globe agree video content has the best return on investment (ROI).

Clearly, adding video marketing to your platforms is something to consider! The connection between author and reader is already personal just based on the nature of the relationship. Adding a welcome video to your website is the perfect way to show your personality to your audience outside of the books you write. We'll cover other types of video marketing later.

Tools You Will Need:

There are many ways to make a welcome video and many tools you can use. I used my Samsung Note phone, a tripod and iMovie software to create my welcome video. I suggest doing a Google search to see what tools you might need based on what you already have on hand.

- ☐ As technology evolves, cameras get cheaper so even if your camera phone doesn't take good video, a camera purchase won't break the bank. (Think Walmart for under $30)
- ☐ A tripod is necessary to keep the video from being shaky even if you have someone to help you.
- ☐ You may need some sort of external microphone depending on the quality of your other equipment. Make sure you don't sound like you are underwater or shouting, and be aware of background noise.
- ☐ A script or bullet point outline of what you want to say.
- ☐ A quiet, well-lit location.
- ☐ Editing software (Don't be frightened… it's not as scary as it sounds!)

Things to Consider and Notes for Your Script:

- ☐ A general greeting such as "Welcome to my page" or "Thanks for stopping by."_____

☐ Who you are — not your whole bio —your name and title or genre.

_____

_____

☐ Anything special or unique about your website or a particular tab.

_____

_____

☐ Include any giveaways or incentives. Don't go into detail — just direct them to where the information can be found.

_____

_____

☐ How can you help them? Remember you aren't trying to sell them anything. You are just answering the door and warmly inviting them into your space.

_____

_____

☐ A call to action (like a reminder to sign up for your email updates or check your calendar for your book event schedule).

_____

_____

Tips for Making a Great Welcome Video:

- TIP: Don't be a talking head. Frame the shots so you can see a portion of your body and be animated.
- TIP: Refer to the advice of what to wear in the *Professional Headshot* task (page 26): no busy patterns, etc.
- TIP: Make your background well lit and purposeful and remember your branding.
- TIP: If you choose music for any portion of your video make sure it is relevant and at a reasonable volume. Music just for the sake of music can be annoying to someone visiting your website. Also, remember you may need permission to use someone else's work so check for usage rights.
- TIP: Your welcome video should be short, sweet, and concise. Keep the time somewhere between 45 seconds and 3 minutes.

Note: This task has two more components: 1) filming 2) post-production.

☐ **Woot woot! Add this completed task to today's calendar!**
☐ **Add to Calendar:** *ASAP Filming*
☐ **Add to Calendar:** *ASAP Post-production*
☐ **Add to Calendar: in 6 months** *repeat all three tasks*

Task: FACEBOOK AUTHOR PAGE
Category: Author Branding

Of all of the social media platforms, Facebook is the most popular with 1.71 billion monthly active users and 1.13 billion daily active users, on average. Facebook also boasts 1.57 billion mobile monthly active users and 1.03 million mobile daily active users, on average. That's a lot of people! It's also important to know the average Facebook visit is 20+ minutes. It would be crazy not to take advantage of such a large audience. We will discuss more statistics that will help you use Facebook (as well as other platforms that may be better suited for your target market) for your particular marketing needs in the **Social Media Marketing** section.

If you already have a personal Facebook profile page, kudos! Skip the step-by-step instructions on how to set it up and just walk through the checklist to make sure you haven't forgotten anything. Make sure all of your information is current. Change up your cover photo, update your social media links or try a different call-to-action button.

Step-by-Step Facebook Profile Page Set-up:
Skip ahead if you already have one. This portion of the task will take about 15 minutes.

To set up a Facebook (FB) author page, you have to have a personal FB profile first. If you have been avoiding being on FB, don't panic! You do not have to use the personal page (though you may decide you want to as we get to other tasks later) and you can put your settings to *private*.

- ☐ Go to www.facebook.com to create a new account. Fill out the required fields and click Create Account. It will take you to new window which will ask you to verify your email.
- ☐ Once you have verified your email, Facebook will walk you through the setup process. It's pretty self-explanatory, but you can come back later to finish setting up your personal page on your personal time. After all, this is your AUTHOR time, not your PERSONAL time— so stay focused and let's get that author page started!

Step-by-Step Facebook Author Page Set-up:
Skip ahead if you already have one. This portion of the task will take about 30 minutes.
Setting up an author page is simpler than you might think!
1. Log into Facebook with the username and password for your personal profile page.

2. In the blue bar at the top of the page, next to the ? (question mark) is a ▼ (downward arrow). Clicking on the arrow will give you a drop-down menu. (Or go to facebook.com/pages/create directly.)
3. Select Create page.
4. Select the Artist, Band or Public Figure option and, again, you will get a drop-down menu with options. Choose Author. Type the name of your new page and click Get started.

   TIP: Remember your branding! Name your page something you can carry across social platforms. Personally, I recommend using your author name with the word *author*. Note: My Facebook author page is facebook.com/pbjauthor, of course.

5. Facebook walks you through the set-up process from there in easy-to-follow steps.

TIP: Facebook will only allow you to change the name of your page once. That's it! Be mindful of typos, don't use the title of your book, and think long term.

TIP: You can create your cover photo in Canva. They have perfectly sized templates!

TIP: Make your profile picture something different from your personal page profile picture to make it easier to distinguish between the two. (How about your snazzy new author headshot?)

TIP: Your description should be some version of your bio as well as your contact info. With Facebook's popularity, readers will often find you there before your website.

TIP: +Add a Button is a great way to get your call to action (CTA) noticed. Direct people to your website to sign up for your email list or direct them to where they can shop for your books.

TIP: Lastly, invite your personal friends who might be interested in your page. While you may occasionally cross-post information, keeping the pages separate by offering different content is important. Those first friends are a great way to start building your following, but remember your personal page is for your personal life and your author page is for your business.

We will cover some of Facebook's features, such as maximizing reach and understanding insights later. For now, just get that page up and running!

☐ **Pat yourself on the back! Add this completed task to today's calendar!**
☐ **Add to Calendar: 3 / 6 / 9** *months from today*

Task: AMAZON AUTHOR PAGE
Category: Author Branding

Love it or hate it, there is no denying Amazon is the world's biggest bookstore and, as such, when it offers you a free platform to share your author information with readers, you should take advantage of it! Whether you have one book or twenty, an Amazon Author Central page is imperative for any author who sells books on the distribution giant's platform.

If you already have an Amazon Author Central page, take the time to go through your information and update it.

Step-by-Step Set-up:
1. Go to https://authorcentral.amazon.com/ to get started.
2. Explore the features of your Amazon page:
   - ☐ Reach more readers
   - ☐ Track sales
   - ☐ Get author assistance
   - ☐ Manage your bibliography
   - ☐ Manage editorial and consumer reviews
   - ☐ Report copyright infringement
3. Follow the tutorial to set up your page.
4. Using information you have gathered for previously completed tasks, consider adding these elements to your page:
   - ☐ Author bio (remember to use 3rd person)
   - ☐ Headshot and other photos
   - ☐ Blog feed
   - ☐ Videos (including book trailers and website welcome video if appropriate)
   - ☐ Events
   - ☐ Awards
   - ☐ Contact info (including website, email, social media links).
   - TIP: Remember to create your custom author page URL to make it easier to promote your Amazon information in places like your media kit.
   - TIP: The customer review tab is a great place to find all of your Amazon reviews in one place to use for marketing!

☐ **You're crushing it! Add this completed task to today's calendar!**
☐ **Add to Calendar: 4 / 8** *months from today*

36

Task: GOODREADS AUTHOR PAGE

Category: Author Branding

Goodreads is the world's largest social network platform for readers and authors. In 2016, there were an estimated 55 million users sharing recommendations, reviews, and discussions about books. The upside for an author is not only can one get in the middle of the conversation but it is another platform putting information in front of very targeted audiences. Goodreads also offers ways for authors to market their books through advertising and giveaways.

It should be noted Goodreads is currently owned by Amazon which means reviews can be cross-promoted.

Step-by-Step Set-up:

1. Signing up for Goodreads is easy! Go to www.goodreads.com and create your free account.
2. Claim your profile..
   - ☐ Author bio
   - ☐ Website links
   - ☐ Reviews
   - ☐ Connect your blog
   - ☐ List your books in the Goodreads database
   - ☐ Answer the *Ask the Author* questions to create interest
3. Connect with friends.

   ☐ TIP: Remember, just like other social platforms, Goodreads is a two-way street, so be sure to review your favorite books and connect with readers and other authors.

*We will talk about advertising on Goodreads in the **Social Media** section.*
*We will talk about networking on Goodreads in the **Networking** section.*

☐ **Sweet! Add this completed task to today's calendar!**
☐ **Add to Calendar: 4 / 8** *months from today*

Task: AUTHOR MEDIA KIT
Category: Author Branding

An author media kit, or press kit, is basic information gathered to give news sources and others the necessary information to write about or promote you. Ideally, your media kit should be short, concise, and provide the viewer with all of the important details they might need. The easier you make it to find your information, the more likely the media will reach out to you and perhaps offer you an opportunity for exposure.

Who might look at your media kit?

- Journalists
- Newscasters
- Bloggers
- Podcasters
- Potential sponsors

Step-by-Step Set-up:

1. Your media kit should be available in three versions:
    - ☐ Display version on a website page
    - ☐ Downloadable version (.pdf file)
    - ☐ Physical version for mailing (may also involve bookmarks or other swag)
2. Things to consider including:
    - ☐ Author name and overview
    - TIP: Refer to your author bio in the Author Branding section and remember to use third person point of view (POV.)
    - ☐ Author headshot
    - ☐ Book synopsis/blurb
    - ☐ Book cover photo
    - ☐ Previous press releases
    - ☐ Media assets (photos, video or audio links, etc.)
    - TIP: Make sure you rename any downloadable files (i.e. "image_345.jpeg" should be "pbj_headshot.jpg" to find easily.)
    - ☐ Awards or distinctions
    - ☐ What is relevant or timely about your book
    - ☐ Provide answers to the most common interview questions
    - ☐ Contact info

☐ **Tired of being awesome yet? Add this completed task to today's calendar!**

☐ **Added to Calendar:** *update 6 months from today*

TAKE A BREAK....

My Superhero name is:

_____

My secret super power is:

_____

_____

Which means I can:

_____

_____

_____

_____

This is what I look like when I'm saving the world:

#creativeweirdos #superheroes #whereismycape

Build Your Tribe

"Call it a clan. Call it a network. Call it a tribe. Call it a family. Whatever you call it, whoever you are, you need one."
Jane Howard

By now you have heard the importance of "building your tribe," but what does it mean? A *tribe* is a group of dedicated fans who support your work and actively help spread your message. Whether your impassioned base is full of beta readers, bloggers, social media followers or just your friends and family, they are the front line of support and belief in you and your journey.

Tribes are usually communities with similar likes and dislikes, dreams, and ambitions. I call the closest of my PJBoox tribe the *Creative Weirdos*, and they (we) are mostly creative types: authors, artists, and musicians. There are other members of the tribe, however, who are not quite as close and even some that I barely know. What they all have in common is a belief that what I am trying to do with the store is worthwhile, and they want to be a part of it. They share posts, retweet, offer me exposure, and show up at events. They refer my business to their friends. They are my secret sauce.

As an author, your tribe will be the people who support, not only your products (books) but the journey you are on as well. You probably have a good start already but wouldn't it be nice to have a few more?

Task: SOCIAL MEDIA FAN BASE
Category: Build Your Tribe

Thanks to the internet, it has become a bit easier to build your tribe. Platforms like social media, online groups, blogs, and podcasts allow you to get your message heard more easily and to find more people who care about it. Growing your tribe organically makes more sense than buying lists of followers since you will already have something in common.

Step-by-Step Set-up:

One of the simplest ways to start connecting with possible tribe members is through Facebook groups.

1. Use the memory jogger on the next page to help you think of groups you might be comfortable in. They do not all have to be related to your book. Rekindling connections with old schoolmates or fraternity brothers will be rewarding in its own right. Book sales will just be a bonus.
2. Use the search tab in Facebook to locate the groups.
3. Read the posted rules of the group before joining or engaging with the members. Some communities (like school or work-related groups) may be only informational and not allow for interaction between group members. Others may require qualifications you don't have.
4. It's okay to lurk a bit before jumping in unless it's a group you already have a connection with like your high school graduating class. In that case, jump right into the conversation!
5. Do not start out by trying to sell your book. Conversations should be natural not sales pitch-y.
6. Be active within the community and contribute.
7. Talk about being an author or your book in subtle ways that fit into normal conversations.
8. Don't get so distracted by participating in social media groups that you lose your focus on writing and marketing.

Maybe it's not a group you can connect with but rather an individual such as an old neighbor or favorite teacher.

1. Spend some time catching up if it's been awhile. Relationship marketing needs to be genuine! You aren't looking to sell books. You are building a tribe of people to help you on the journey.
2. Remember, communication is a two way street. It can't always be about you.

X	Group	Facebook link
	High school alumni	
	College alumni	
	Fraternity / Sorority	
	Professional affiliations	
	Clubs	
	Church	
	Hobbies	
	Military	
	Athletic groups	
	Parents groups	
	Local business groups	
	Other	

X	Personal	Name	Name
	Neighbors		
	Book club		
	Wine club		
	Leaders (teachers, etc.)		
	Support group		
	Volunteer groups		
	Current co-workers		
	Previous co-workers		
	Business Owners		
	Others		

☐ **What determination! Add this completed task to today's calendar!**

☐ **Add to Calendar:** *Add a new group every month = 12x. Leave groups that no longer work for you.*

Task: EMAIL LIST
Category: Build Your Tribe

Your email list is one more way for you to communicate with your tribe. Hard as it may be to believe, not everyone you know is on social media platforms, but almost every one has email. Not convinced of the power of email yet? Here are some statistics about email marketing, according to Constant Contact (an email marketing company):

1. 205 billion emails are sent every day.
2. Email has a higher conversion rate than social media.
3. 72% of consumers state they prefer email as their source of business communication.
4. 61% of consumers enjoy getting promotional emails weekly. 38% would like emails to come even more frequently.

We will talk about how to best use email for marketing in the General Marketing section (page 114) but now let's talk about building the list. Your email list is a valuable asset!

See also: The CAN-SPAM Act: https://www.ftc.gov/tips-advice/business-center/guidance/can-spam-act-compliance-guide-business for guidance on requirements for commercial messages.

The Checklist for Building Your List Organically:

- ☐ Add a sign-up form to your website offering a newsletter or something else of value (free ebook, report, newsletter, industry tips, etc.)
- ☐ Add a *Sign Up* call-to-action (CTA) from your YouTube videos, Facebook author page, and other social media platforms.
- ☐ Create a guest book to take to events. People are more comfortable giving you their information if they meet you in person, so events are a GREAT time to list build.

  TIP: Differentiate emails from different events to target those email recipients specifically if you do the same or similar event in the future.
- ☐ Create a giveaway contest. Collect email addresses in exchange for a chance to win.

  TIP: You can make a ballot box from a shoe box or even a bowl.
- ☐ Split your content into *general* and *needs email sign-in* categories.

  TIP: Include wording to assure people you will not spam them.

Google top-ranked email platforms: MailChimp, Constant Contact, and Drip. All have free (or free trial) options as well as monthly paid upgrades. Plan for growth.

- ☐ Fantastic! Add this completed task to today's calendar!
- ☐ *Update regularly!*

Task: STREET TEAM
Category: Build Your Tribe

So you have joined groups online and have reconnected with people from your past. Now what?

The Checklist:

1. Getting started:
   - [ ] Invite your tribe to like and follow you on your social media platforms.
   - [ ] Add them to your email list.
   - [ ] Sort tribe members into two groups:
     - [ ] Readers: People who will purchase your books and show up at your events.
     - [ ] Street team: Fans who will voluntarily support you via word-of-mouth, active social media sharing, beta reading, ARC (Advance Reading Copies) reviews and more.
   - TIP: Create a separate Facebook group to communicate with your street team.

2. Managing your street team:
   - [ ] Consider sending them a Street Team Kit which might include bookmarks, marketing materials, buttons, or other SWAG.
   - TIP: Start with a smaller, more intimate number and grow organically. Let the members of the team come up with a name for the group.
   - [ ] Organize specific challenges or tasks for them to do weekly or monthly. These might include:
     - [ ] Posting reviews.
     - [ ] Establishing contact with local retailers/bookstores/libraries.
     - [ ] Dispensing your marketing materials at events.
     - [ ] Leaving comments on blog sites when you are featured.
   - [ ] Create a points or prize system to reward the members of your street team for their hard work!
   - TIP: Sometimes the cool reward is not stuff but rather time with you. Do scheduled Facebook live videos so you can interact with the team.
   - [ ] Use your team for brainstorming character names, cover options, and other places you might need reader feedback.

- [ ] **Whoop! There it is! Add this completed task to today's calendar!**

- [ ] **Add to Calendar:** *Engage with your street team regularly but task them once a month (12x), bi-weekly (24x) or weekly (52x)*

Events

**"They may forget what you said,
but they will never forget how you made them feel."**
Carl W. Buechner

A professionally designed cover and a well-written blurb will intrigue readers and you can also count on bookstore/retail staff to hand-sell your books … but, realistically, nothing sells a book better than you, the author, in a public setting! The connection between author and reader can be very intense in person, and a reader who feels a personal connection to an author is more likely to not only support the work but persuade others to do the same.

One of the common factors among independent authors is a certain shyness to speaking or appearing in public to promote their books. While it isn't mandatory to self-promote in person, this workbook will explore some of the ways that an author can better prepare for in-person events, become more confident, and sell more books!

The theme, venue, display, and even the guest list can be influenced by branding, genre or timing. Each event, whether a solo effort or a huge festival, should be carefully planned and promoted. Preparation is key so let's get started…

Note: The tasks in this section will lead to twelve events over the next year: two festival events, three podcasts, four bookstore/retail events and one book club event. Obviously, even more events can lead to even more exposure and book sales. Don't limit yourself to one a month…just go for it!

Task: EVENT PLANNING
Category: Events

Note: This task is listed as free, however, there may be optional components that do require fees such as festival fees, marketing materials, or travel expenses.

There is a lot to do in the planning of an author event, but direct contact with potential readers is almost always worth it. The more events you do, the more comfortable you will get with your display, presentation, and audience interaction.

The Checklist:
1. What type of event are you planning?
   - General venue:
     - ☐ Author presentation: authors expound on their subject matter with a slide show or powerpoint and speak in front of the group, often with a book signing to follow.
     - ☐ New book launch party: a celebration of a new book release and probably one of the most profitable events when done properly.
     - ☐ Fundraiser/Charity event: the author may donate a portion of sales or donate product. Authors may participate for exposure and not monetary gain.
   - Festival:
     - ☐ Book festival/fair: generally a multi-author event held outdoors or in a large conference area. Costs can be $0 — $300+
   - Bookstore:
     - ☐ Author signing: the traditional author signing copies of his/her books.
   - Media:
     - ☐ Podcast interviews, television, or radio appearances: generally promotional not necessarily directly income producing.
   - School:
     - ☐ School visit: the standard for children's book, or even YA, authors. Authors may charge speaker fees or book sales or both.
   - Speaking engagements:
     - ☐ Workshop: an educational, interactive group setting with the author as an expert and the audience participating in a learning environment. Speaking fees and/or books sales may be generated.
   - Book Clubs:
     - ☐ Readers groups: in person or via video chat creates a direct channel of communication between authors and readers.

- Other:
  - ☐ Virtual book party: from the comfort of your own home, possibly in your pajamas! This would be for exposure which would hopefully translate to book sales.

2. Selecting a venue (make notes as you brainstorm):

☐ Bookstore _____

_____

☐ Retail location _____

_____

☐ Restaurant _____

_____

☐ Clubhouse _____

_____

☐ Church _____

_____

☐ Airport _____

_____

☐ Library _____

_____

☐ Coffeehouse _____

_____

☐ Genre-inspired setting (If your book is about a train, maybe have your event on a train?) _____

_____

☐ A location mentioned in your book _____

_____

_____

☐ Other ideas _____

_____

_____

_____

TIP: Select the date and time by focusing on your target audience. When would they be most likely to attend your event?

3. What's in it for the venue? _____

_____

4. Things to remember when contacting the venue:

☐ Point of contact _____

☐ Date _____ Alt date _____

☐ Time _____ to _____
☐ Cost _____
☐ What is provided? (tables, etc.) _____

_____
☐ Amount of space is available _____
☐ Are refreshments...
    ☐ provided?
    ☐ BYO?
    ☐ restricted?
    ☐ able to be dropped off early?

TIP: Contact the venue and nail down the date as soon as possible.

5. Marketing and Promotion: Determine who will do...
    1) the Facebook event page _____ Author _____ Venue _____ N/A
    2) press release to the media _____ Author _____ Venue _____ N/A
    3) posters _____ Author _____ Venue _____ N/A
    4) postcards _____ Author _____ Venue _____ N/A
    5) email blasts _____ Author _____ Venue _____ N/A
    6) online local calendars _____ Author _____ Venue _____ N/A
    7) direct mail _____ Author _____ Venue _____ N/A

6. How is the inventory being handled?
    ☐ Pre-ordered by venue through distribution (Ingram, etc)
    ☐ Supplied by publisher
    ☐ Supplied by author

7. How is the money being handled?
    ☐ Pre-ordered by venue through distribution (Ingram, etc)
    ☐ Consignment of _____% to Author _____% to Venue
    ☐ Venue handles sale transactions and payout to author in _____days
    ☐ Author handles sales transactions

TIP: Remember if you are traveling somewhere, look to see if you can add an
    author event while you are there. It may expose your work to a new
    audience and may make portions of your trip tax-deductible (consult your
    accountant).

☐ **Remarkable! Add this completed task to today's calendar!**
Use the chart on the next page to schedule all the tasks you have to do for a general
venue event. Check the Table of Contents for other event pages.

Tasks for GENERAL VENUE Event	Add to calendar	#1	#2	#3	#4
Date of event	Date of event				
Press release	3 weeks prior to event				
Send marketing materials	3 weeks prior to event				
FB event page	2 weeks prior to event				
Email blast	1-2 weeks prior				
Venue check-in	3 days prior to event				
Post-event tasks	1 day after event				

NOTES: _____

_____

_____

_____

_____

_____

_____

Task: MEDIA LIST
Category: Events

* *Note: This task is listed as free, however, some optional components may require a fee.* An updated list of local media outlets is essential in building your brand through events and news releases. Media lists should include: newsprint, magazines, radio, television, and bloggers.

The Checklist:

1. Remember your target audience when creating your list. Who is your ideal buyer and which media sources would best reach them? _____

    _____

    _____

    TIP: Use USNPL.com to find links to newspapers and TV stations in the United States —including colleges!

2. You can purchase a list. I have used http://www.easymedialist.com/ and was happy with the results. I was able to narrow down my selections to 16 news sources and spent $24. It was well worth getting a reliable list without spending the time to do the research on my own. Google <your town + media list> to find other resources.

Outlet	Contact	Title	Email	Phone	Notes

☐ **Phew! That was a good one! Add this completed task to today's calendar!**
Press release scheduling can be found on specific event scheduling pages.

Task: PRESS RELEASE
Category: Events

* *Note: This task is listed as free. However, I do recommend having the press release professionally edited, preferably by someone who is an expert in PRs and there will likely be a cost involved. Do it anyway.*

A press release is generally a written communication that a business or organization sends to members of the press. It can be used to share information about the business, announce news or promote an event. As an authorpreneur, you might create a press release to announce a new book release, pairing with a charity or topical cause, celebrating an accolade or promoting an event.

The Checklist for Writing a Great Press Release:

What makes a press release successful? When the publication or news source takes your press release information and shares it to the public, I'd call that a success. If the news story is picked up by other sources (blogs, online news, websites and social media), I'd call that a VERY successful press release!

- ☐ Write in the third person.
- ☐ Tell an interesting story. Would you want to attend your event based on the press release? Outline what's in it for the audience. There's a lot of competition out there. Make sure your event sounds worth the reader's time.
- ☐ Keep it short and succinct (no more than two printed pages).
- ☐ Single space your finished press release. Double space your press release if it will need copy editing.
- ☐ Add a call to action (link to buy tickets, visit website, get more information,
- ☐ Send your PR out 2 - 3 weeks before your event.
- ☐ Check your media list (page 52) for direct contacts (lifestyle reporter, etc.) via email and physical address. It's okay to be old school and send a printed copy! News people are busy reading content on their computer all day so an envelope on their desk might just be different enough to get noticed. If you do send a physical copy, reference your email so they know they can cut and paste the copy.
- ☐ Start with local media and then leverage any success to go regionally or even nationally.
- ☐ Include a link to your media kit (page 38).
- ☐ Write the PR like a news story and the news source is more likely to use it since they don't have to do as much work to include it. You can also present it as an interview with Q&A.

Sample press release:

13550 Reflections Pkwy, Fort Myers, 33907

Patti Brassard Jefferson, CEO
P.J. Boox Bookstore

FOR IMMEDIATE RELEASE

Fort Myers: Home to the largest independent author bookstore in the U.S.

Forget what your mother told you, it's okay to judge a book by its cover!

FORT MYERS, Fla. – Jan 17, 2016 - Fort Myers has long been known as a haven for artists of all mediums and now, hundreds of independent authors from all over the world can call it home, thanks to award-winning author and illustrator, Patti Brassard Jefferson, and her new bookstore, *P.J. Boox*.

Open since October 2015, this unique bookstore is one of the few booksellers in the country who exclusively sell the works of independent or small press published authors. Jefferson came up with the idea of a larger store with a global reach months after opening the *Gulf Coast Bookstore* with business partner, Tim Jacobs, in Downtown Fort Myers. At the time, *Publisher's Weekly* touted the store as the "first bookstore dedicated to self-published authors," though the idea quickly grew more popular and a couple of indie-only bookstores popped up across the country. Jefferson decided to expand the arena for indie authors within her new store. Currently she has opened the door to over 260 authors representing 11 countries including the UK, Canada, New Zealand, Australia, Israel and Jamaica. When at full capacity, over 500 authors will be able to display their books in over 1,600 square feet of retail space.

Not only is the bookstore concept unique, but the way in which the books are displayed on their shelves is novel as well. The front-facing displays instantly draw in potential readers as they are able to, quite literally, judge a book by its cover. Each author has a floating wall shelf to showcase their books and readers are encouraged to pick up the display books, read the blurbs and flip through the pages. Pristine copies are kept in bookcases under the wall displays. "A title on a spine from an unknown author isn't going to sell a book. Readers are drawn in with the cover. We invite them to pick up and hold the book and that makes a connection more comfortable," says Jefferson.

Industry experts have reported that small bookstores will need to offer more of a "customer experience" to stay afloat in the digital age. P.J. Boox agrees. While it is has become somewhat traditional for a bookstore to have a designated reading section, P.J. Boox uses their reading space to enhance the reader experience in a new way. Whether it's a Saturday Kids Club event or book club meeting, the readers can actually interact with the author of the featured book in real time via Skype or other video chat option. Being able to connect authors and readers directly takes the entire book experience to a deeper level.

Of course, since P.J. Boox features books from all over the globe, it makes sense for them to be able to reach readers all over the globe as well. In December 2015, P.J. Boox launched a new website (www.pjboox.com) full of author information, reader reviews, discussion forums and, of course, books for sale. A weekly blog and e-books options will be added in February.

Independent authors have called Jefferson a "disrupter" of the traditional bookseller industry and it's a title she wears like a badge of honor. "Sometimes cages need to be rattled," says Jefferson. "Today's readers don't always want to be told what to read. They are discovering new authors on their own. We just decided to make that quest easier." Jefferson points to a quote by Haruki Murakami on the wall of the bookstore - "If you only read the books everyone else is reading, you can only think whatever one else is thinking." She smiles. "That just about sums up P.J. Boox."

P.J. Boox Hours of operation:
Monday - Friday 10 am - 7 pm
Saturday 10 am - 6 pm
Sunday Noon - 5 pm

For more information: www.pjboox.com

Patti Brassard Jefferson - 239-437-3227, pjboox@gmail.com

!!!!!! ###

① Address and company name

② State "For Immediate Release" or add release date

③ Headline and sub-head

④ Show local relevance

⑤ Cite known experts

⑥ Use reliable statistics

⑦ Have a creative hook

⑧ Contact info including phone, email, website and even social media links

TIP: Attach high-resolution professional photos to press release emails to make them convenient for reporters to access.

Press Release Template:

☐ Headline: Sum up the focus of the press release in less than 20 words.

_____
_____
_____

☐ Subhead _____
_____

☐ City, State - Month Day, Year _____

☐ Attention Grabber: Intriguing first sentence _____
_____
_____

☐ Description of event, award, or news _____
_____
_____
_____

☐ Interesting and relevant quotes _____
_____
_____

☐ Local or current event tie in _____
_____

☐ Call to action (CTA) _____
_____

☐ Contact Info _____
_____

☐ About the author (short bio) _____
_____

☐ **You're making this look easy! Add this completed task to today's calendar!**
Press release scheduling can be found on specific event scheduling pages.

Task: PRE-EVENT PROMOTION
Category: Events

So you have a date booked with the venue for your event, so now what? You need to get the word out so that you have a great turn out and sell a boatload of books!

The Checklist:
Here are some of the things you should be doing before your event that will help you get ready and help with your promotions.

1. Get the event listed on online event calendars:
   - ☐ Google <venue city + calendar>, and you will likely find a number of calendars where you can post your event.
   - ☐ Remember to use a graphic (author headshot, book cover, etc.) if possible.
   - ☐ Include the date and time, the address of the venue, and any ticket or RSVP information.
   - ☐ Add your website link.
   - ☐ WHEN: Can be done as soon as the date and time are set.

2. Create a press release (page 53):
   - ☐ WHEN: Information should be submitted to daily papers two weeks before the event.
   - ☐ Target the lifestyle or entertainment sections.
   - ☐ WHEN: Monthly magazines usually have deadlines two or three weeks before the start of the next month so confirm their deadline.
   - ☐ TV news outlets all have websites that will have lists of people to contact regarding news and events. Some promotional "morning show" type setups will have a cost for the advertiser (that's you).

3. Get marketing materials to the venue (some of these may not apply to all venues):
   - ☐ Postcards (page 124) at the checkout counter of the venue or used as bag stuffers with purchase.
   - ☐ Find out how many places, if any, the venue has for posters (page 128)
   - ☐ Other signage and items for a display if they have room. Consider giving the staff of the venue free copies of the book so they can find out more about your book and be able to talk about it.

4. If the venue doesn't do a Facebook event page, make one from your author page. (see page 58)

☐ WHEN: One to two weeks seems to be the sweet spot to start promoting through a FB event: longer and people procrastinate, shorter and they don't have enough time to plan.

5. Make announcements (posts, tweets, etc.) on social media:
   ☐ Facebook author page
   ☐ Twitter
   ☐ Other
   ॒ TIP: Don't just continually blast that you have the event. Be subtle: post pictures of your new banner when it arrives or the shoes you bought for the occasion.
   ॒ TIP: Remember that graphics and videos get more traction.

6. Send out an email blast (ask the venue to do the same):
   ☐ To your newsletter subscribers (email list)
   ☐ To blog followers
   ॒ TIP: Send the venue contact a pre-written email for them to send. Not having to create content themselves will save them time.

7. Co-op an advertisement with the venue:
   ☐ Direct mailer campaign.
   ☐ Print ad in publication

8. Who else might attend?
   ☐ Use your information from the **Identify Your Audience** task on page 16.
   ☐ Look for groups or organizations that would have an interest in your subject matter and contact them.
   ॒ TIP: Consider offering them a free copy that they can use as a giveaway in exchange for an email blast to their members or a newsletter mention.
   ☐ Brainstorming:_____

9. Touch base with the venue a couple of days before to find out response to the event and to make sure everything is going as planned.

10. Put out a last minute push on all platforms a day or two ahead.

☐ **You are really rocking this! Add this completed task to today's calendar!**
Pre-event promotion scheduling can be found on specific event scheduling pages.

Task: FACEBOOK EVENT PAGE
Category: Events

Social media is a great place to let people know about upcoming events. Facebook has made it easy to set up a dedicated page (linked to your author page) to promote your events. If you are participating in an event that someone else is hosting, they will probably have an event page that you can share. Setting up an event page of your own gives you a way to reach your event subscribers directly and increase awareness of your event.

Step-by-Step Set-up

1. Go to your author page and select Events from the column on the left under your profile picture.
2. Click on +Create Event.
   - TIP: You can create a graphic for your event in Canva using the *Facebook Event* template.
   - TIP: You can also use a video for your event header which will grab even more attention!
3. Fill in the applicable fields and click Publish when done (or Schedule if you want to release it in the future. Make sure you offer as much information as possible to potential attendees.
4. https://events.fb.com is the Facebook tutorial on creating your event page and will, undoubtedly, have the most up to date information.
5. Consider allowing attendees to buy tickets from your event page, if applicable, which should increase ticket sales for almost any event.
6. There are a couple of ways to share events for better reach:
   1. Invite friends individually from the Share button on your event page. Encourage your fanbase to also invite friends the same way.
   2. Share in your news feed (also from the Share button menu).
   3. Boost the post. There is a small cost for this, but the plus is that you can target your market and reach outside of your existing fanbase.
7. Post to the event page regularly leading up to the event and encourage interaction so that Facebook algorithms will increase your reach.
   - TIP: Event pages should be created two weeks ahead of the event for maximum exposure. People need time to plan but you don't want it to be so far off that they forget.

☐ **Success! Add this completed task to today's calendar!**

Facebook event page scheduling can be found on specific event scheduling pages.

Task: EVENT PROMOTION ONLINE

Category: Events

There are many places to promote your events, and the internet is one of the easiest ways to reach people outside of your existing fanbase without breaking the bank. Use this task page to help you figure out the places that might work best for your event.

The Checklist:

☐ Search <event promotion + my city> in the Facebook search bar. Check the results out to find Groups and Pages that might benefit you to participate in.

☐ Using your results from the *Identify your Audience* section (see page 15), create other keywords to search for relevant Pages or Groups through Facebook's search bar.

☐ Use Google to run the searches on <my city + event calendar>.

☐ Craigslist.com has an events category.

☐ You can create an event page on LinkedIn and invite your connections.

☐ Incentivize your followers to share your event information on social platforms (i.e., a prize for inviting the most people).

☐ Create an email invitation through programs like Constant Contact and digital card platforms like evite.com. Snazzy graphics can change a ho-hum email invitation into something special!

☐ Use paid advertising on social platforms. Take time to learn how the ads work and aim for a very specifically targeted reach. Do not spend a lot of money on ads until you have an idea of how to maximize your return on investment (ROI).

☐ Other ideas:

_____

_____

_____

_____

_____

_____

☐ **Keep going! Add this completed task to today's calendar!**

Online promotion scheduling can be found on specific event scheduling pages.

Task: THE EVENT BAG
Category: Events

Preparing for events can be challenging and hectic, especially if you aren't prepared. Create and maintain an event bag: gather supplies before the event, pack the bag, and restock right after the event to ensure that you are prepared for the next one.

Obviously, not all events are the same, but the checklist below has all of the essentials that you need to have for most events. *Note: Tents, tables, and chairs are not included.*

The Checklist:

☐ **The bag** itself should be on wheels for ease of transportation. The first time you have to park three blocks from the venue and make six trips back and forth to your vehicle, you will be grateful for having a well stocked event bag that you can pull behind you. Outside pockets or compartments are helpful. *Prices will vary.*

> 💡 TIP: Thrift stores are a great place to find wheeled suitcases at reasonable prices!

☐ **Tablecloth** I use a six foot spandex tablecloth that I purchased from a wedding supply company on-line. It has "pockets" that the table legs fit in which is perfect for outdoor events. These come in a variety of colors (think author branding) and some companies will even customize them with your logo. Spandex is also wrinkle-free so your table always looks neat and professional. Each tablecloth fits into a gallon Ziploc bag to keep it orderly in the event bag.

☐ **Signage** can be a variety of things, including a standing banner, hanging banner, author/book info on foam core, etc. If it can be rolled up or folded and added to your bag, it will save you having to carry one extra thing!

☐ **Pricing sheets** are necessary so that people know right away what the cost is. Often at events, authors will offer "bundled" deals and it's good to make that clear in case you are busy talking to someone else and can't immediately share that information with a browser.

☐ **Survival kit**: bandaids, bug spray, lip balm, sunscreen, hand sanitizer, aspirin, deodorant, toothbrush, hairbrush, protein bars/snacks.

☐ **T-shirt / accessories** can be stored in your event bag so they will be clean and ready to go after you are done setting up your space and need to change.

☐ **Guest books** can be very fancy or just discount store notebooks. The whole point of the guest book is to build your email list of fans who would be interested in your other events or specials. Your list is invaluable.

TIP: Start a fresh page with the event location and date labeled at the top. Sorting your email list geographically makes it easier to promote in that area in the future.

- ☐ **Giveaway box** and ballot slips are a good way to build your email list.
- ☐ **Office supplies** can be kept in a plastic pencil box or lunch box. Some items you might consider including are: pens/pencils, extra sharpies, index cards, scissors, various types of tape, stapler, pushpins, and paper clips.
- ☐ **Post-it notes** are another office supply that you shouldn't be without, because sometimes Bob is actually spelled "B-A-H-B" and you will want to know that before you sign the book.

  TIP: Hand the sticky note to the buyer and have THEM write the name to avoid any misunderstanding of challenging spellings.

- ☐ **Marketing materials** you should have on hand include: branded bookmarks and business cards (and some sort of holder for them), posters and any SWAG. *See Marketing materials.*
- ☐ **Credit card swiper** from PayPal or Square (free with your account) for taking credit and debit cards with your smart phone is a necessity! Don't lose sales because the buyer doesn't have cash.
- ☐ **Name tag/lanyard**
- ☐ **Book stands/racks** to display your books.
- ☐ **Tiles** for leveling tables that are sitting in holes. *Note: I carry ceramic tiles.*
- ☐ **Spare phone/tablet charging cord** with USB plug.
- ☐ **Hat/visor**
- ☐ **Spare reading glasses**
- ☐ **Windbreaker** for weather changes including drop in temperature, wind, or rain.
- ☐ **Twine/bungie cord**
- ☐ **Clear bags for purchases** so folks can see your book as the buyer walks around!
- ☐ **Extension cord and power strip** (if applicable)

Checklist for things not kept in the bag:
- ☐ **Small cooler** for bottled water and snacks.
- ☐ **USB phone charger** fully charged.
- ☐ **Cash**
- ☐ **Smart phone** fully charged.

☐ **Well, well... look at you! Add this completed task to today's calendar!**

Task: DURING AND AFTER EVENT

Category: Events

So you booked an event and have gathered all the things you need from the *Event Bag* task (page 60). Now what? This task page has some tips for what to do while at your event and also a checklist of what to do AFTER the event.

During the Event Tips:

- TIP: Don't sit behind a table. Be approachable. To the reader, part of the magic of meeting an author is the personal connection.

- TIP: Take a couple of photos before the event starts and share on your social platforms, then turn your phone off. Engage with the potential customers around you. You only need your phone for credit card transactions.

- TIP: Encourage attendees to take selfies with you and your book whether they buy from you or not. If they share to their tribe, you may reach potential buyers who are not even at the event. Make it easy for them to tag you.

- TIP: Encourage people to sign your guest book or to enter your giveaway.

- TIP: If it is a multi-author event (festival, etc.), take time to look at other author displays. Make note of what is eye-catching or seems to draw people in and do that next time.

- TIP: Be smart with your SWAG (page 130).

After the Event Checklist:

☐ Post pictures of the event on your social media platforms.

☐ Announce the winner of your giveaway with some fanfare.

☐ Enter all of the emails in your mail account. Send an email thank you with a call to action (visit website, follow on social media, etc.)
- TIP: Create folders for different events so that you can reach out to those customers directly when you are coming back next year.

☐ Restock your event bag. Replace anything you used or stock anything you realized you forgot. Have it ready to go for the next event.

□ Send a hand-written thank you note to the venue or event coordinator. It will make an impression and, even if the event didn't go as well as expected, they will be more inclined to invite you back and to also hand-sell any books you may have left behind in inventory.

□ Do a post-event summary. By tracking actual facts about events, you will be able to analyze which events were worth attending and which ones you can skip in the future. Author budgets are always aided by hard data, so get in the habit of looking at the numbers and making smart business decisions.

Event	Date / Time	Cost of event	Other expenses (travel, etc.)	Est. attendance	Number of books sold	Income

□ **Time for your happy dance! Add this completed task to today's calendar!**

Task: FESTIVAL LIST
Category: Events

Book fairs, multi-author events, and other creative festivals may be some of the best ways to promote your books in person. These opportunities to get in front of your targeted market can be an excellent way to engage with readers and build your fanbase, as well as generate book sales, of course!

There are a lot of things to consider when deciding which events to participate in:
- Location - How far away is it and is it in a location that makes sense for your genre?
- Dates - Does the event conflict with other obligations you have?
- Past attendance - How long has the event been around and what has the previous attendance been?
- Promotion - How is the event promoted (traditionally and socially)?
- Registration - What are the costs and the deadlines? What are the policies if you have to cancel or if the event gets canceled?

Here is a list of some online resources you can use to start creating your list:
- EverFest - https://www.everfest.com/book-festivals
- The African American Library Book Club - http://aalbc.com/events/
- Book Reporter - http://www.bookreporter.com/book-festivals
- Publishing Events Around the World - www.bookfestivals.com

TIP: For events near you, search <state + book festival> (example: Florida book festivals).

TIP: Also search for any subjects that may connect with your book (example: children's events, art/craft shows, trade shows, historical reenactments, cultural events, etc.)

TIP: Subscribe to your local and regional online calendars so you don't miss some smaller but profitable events.

The List:
Start with basic research and use the chart on the next page to list as many festivals as may be relevant. Even if you can't afford the time or the money for more than one or two this year, gathering information now will save you time later.

TIP: Think about events close to you to avoid extra travel and lodging expenses.

TIP: Consider festivals that take place somewhere you enjoy visiting.

Festival	City/St	Date	Attend #	Cost	Reg Deadline	Contact
Miami Book Fair	Miami, FL	Nov 17-19, 2017	250k	$300	July 30, 2017	ghernan3@mdc.edu

☐ **Cheers to you! Add this completed task to today's calendar!**

Task: FESTIVAL EVENT
Category: Events

**Refer to Festival list on previous page.

The Checklist:

1. Is it inside or outside? _____

2. What is the cancellation policy due to weather? _____

3. How many attendees are expected? _____

4. What sort of marketing is being done to promote the event? _____

   _____

5. Are there any additional ways you can promote the event? _____

   _____

6. Are there any restrictions to what and when you can sell? _____

   _____

- 💡 TIP: If the event allows, reach out to other authors you know who might be willing to split expenses with you.
- 💡 TIP: Don't forget to post the event on your social media and start creating buzz.
- 💡 TIP: Read the pre-event information in the **Events** section.
- 💡 TIP: When possible reach out to participants of the previous year's event to get their feedback, however understand that everyone's experiences may be different based on numerous factors.

CHALLENGE: *Add one or two events to your calendar depending on your time flexibility and budget.*

☐ **One step closer to the end! Add this completed task to today's calendar !**
Use the chart on the next page to schedule all the tasks you have to do for a venue event. Check them off once you add them to the calendars.

Tasks for FESTIVAL Event	Schedule on calendar	#1	#2
Date of event	Date of event		
Registration	1 month prior to event		
Press release	3 week prior to event		
Email blast	1-2 weeks prior		
Post-event tasks	1 day after event		

NOTES: _____

_____

_____

_____

_____

_____

_____

_____

_____

_____

TAKE A BREAK....

My pirate name:

_____

My pirate ship's name:

_____

My trusty parrot's name:

_____

The 5 best things about being raised by pirates:

1. _____
_____

2. _____
_____

3. _____
_____

4. _____
_____

5. _____
_____

#creativeweirdos #piratelife #whyistherumalwaysgone

Task: PODCAST LIST
Category: Events

Defining what podcasts are is probably a good place to start. A podcast is essentially a talk radio show that you listen to on demand on the internet. It's usually a series of audio episodes with a certain theme. Listeners can subscribe to specific podcasts and then listen to them live or recorded.

So what does that mean for an author? Being on a popular podcast could provide the author with some fantastic exposure and the opportunity to build a larger fanbase. So how do you find the right podcasts?

How-to Steps:
1. Ideas for building your podcast list:
   - ☐ Get recommendations from other authors you know.
   - ☐ Google <podcast for authors>.
   - ☐ Refer to the authors you listed as your "competition" (page 15) and search for them in iTunes to see podcasts they have been on.
2. Ideas for fine tuning your podcast list. Only pick the ones that meet your criteria:
   - ☐ Have they published an episode lately?
   - ☐ Do they publish on a regular schedule?
   - ☐ Is it a good match for you and your brand?
   - ☐ Do they do author interviews?
   - ☐ Do they have a large following? If you can't find a number, how many followers do they have on other social platforms?
3. Create a spreadsheet to reference when you are ready to book a podcast event.

Podcast URL	Email	# of Subscribers	Theme	Notes for Reference

☐ **Wow! Just wow! Add this completed task to today's calendar!**

Task: PODCAST EVENT

Category: Events

Using your Podcast list on the previous page, let's talk about how to get booked as a guest on a podcast.

The Checklist:

1. Be familiar with their podcast:
   - ☐ Read the *About* page
   - ☐ Listen to a couple of episodes

2. Make a list of topics you feel qualified to discuss:

   _____
   _____
   _____
   _____
   _____
   _____

3. What's in it for the podcast? Why do you think their audience would be interested in hearing from you?

   _____
   _____
   _____
   _____

4. Draft an email. Google <podcast pitch template> for inspiration.

5. Have your editor go over your email before you send it.

   💡 TIP: Remember that you are on the podcast to add value for the subscribers. Selling your book should be a natural by-product, but not your focus.

   💡 TIP: Don't feel qualified or don't have the time to book a podcast yourself? Google <podcast booking service> for options that work for you. (Psst - there are also free services available in that Google search.)

☐ **You are doing great!! Add this completed task to today's calendar!**
Use the chart on the next page to schedule all the tasks you have to do for a podcast event. Check them off once you add them to the calendars.

Tasks for PODCAST Event	Schedule on calendar	#1	#2	#3
Date of event	Date of event			
Email blast	1-2 weeks prior			
Social media blast	2 days prior			
Post-event tasks	1 day after event			

NOTES: _____

_____

_____

_____

_____

_____

_____

_____

_____

_____

Task: BOOKSTORE LIST
Category: Events

Author signings, presentations, and book launch parties are a staple at independent bookstores, and the relationships between authors and bookstores is invaluable. Creating a list of bookstore resources will make scheduling a book tour easier.

Here is a list of some online resources you can use to start creating your list:
- Bookstores in the US and Canada - https://www.newpages.com/independent-bookstores
- IndieBound - https://www.indiebound.org/indie-bookstore-finder *Note: this list includes American Bookstore Association members only*

TIP: Search <state + bookstore> (example: Florida bookstores) to find independent bookstores near you.

TIP: NEVER reach out to a bookstore until you have checked out their website and social media platforms for author submission guidelines.

TIP: Form an actual relationship with your local bookstore. Good testimonials from them will give you more leverage when approaching other stores.

TIP: Plan bookstore visits to coincide with your travel plans.

TIP: Network with other authors in your area to get recommendations.

The List:
Use the chart to start with basic research. You don't need to add anything to the calendars until you have booked a bookstore event. As you learn about other bookstore locations, add them to the list. This will become a valuable resource for years to come.

Gathering information now will save you time later. Obviously, the more bookstore events you can schedule, the better. Committing to reaching out to at least one bookstore every month is a good place to start.

Bookstore	Type	City/St	Website	Phone	Submiss. Process	Contact
PJ Boox	Indie only	Fort Myers, FL	pjboox.net	239-437-3227	online	Patti Jefferson

☐ **Work hard! Dream big! Add this completed task to today's calendar!**

Task: BOOKSTORE EVENT
Category: Events

Bookstores are run by people who love books. You write books. Sounds like a no-brainer that you should do an event in a bookstore!

The Checklist:

1. Use the list you created (page 73) to contact some bookstores about hosting an event for you.
   - ☐ Of course, the first bookstore you approach should be the local store where you buy books. Since you already have a relationship with the owner, they are much more likely to agree to have your event.
   - 💡 TIP: Get a testimonial from your local bookseller after your event so that you can use it when you approach other booksellers in the future
   - ☐ Visit the bookstore website to see if they have a page of author information.
   - ☐ If you can't find the information, call the store and ask what their process or policy is for author events. *Note: Email is not as effective.*
   - ☐ Speak to the bookstore owner in person if possible (another good reason to start local).
   - ☐ Remember… your author event has to be worthwhile for both you AND the venue. They are not in the business of doing authors favors, so make sure you explain what makes you a draw.
   - ☐ Let them know your marketing plans for this event.
   - ☐ Do not send unsolicited copies of your books (it's an unnecessary expense).
   - ☐ Know your audience, and be able to discuss it with the venue contact so they know what to expect and where they may be able to help you.
   - 💡 TIP: Getting into Barnes & Noble: Talk to the local store manager. Not all events have to go through corporate approval, but be prepared to navigate the corporate process outlined on their website (www.bn.com).

CHALLENGE: Use this task at least four times to schedule bookstore events this year!

☐ **Winner, winner! Chicken dinner! Add this completed task to today's calendar!**
Use the chart on the next page to schedule all the tasks you have to do for a bookstore event. Check them off once you add them to the calendars.

Tasks for GENERAL VENUE Event	Add to calendar	#1	#2	#3	#4
Date of event	Date of event				
Press release	3 weeks prior to event				
Send marketing materials	3 weeks prior to event				
Facebook event page	2 weeks prior to event				
Email blast	1-2 weeks prior				
Bookstore check-in	3 days prior to event				
Post-event tasks	1 day after event				

NOTES: _____

_____

_____

_____

_____

_____

_____

_____

Task: SCHOOL LIST

Category: Events

At first glance, it may seem that this task is strictly for children's book authors. However, authors of almost every genre can do school visits and talk about the writing process or curriculum-specific topics, especially to the higher grade levels. Educators are always looking for ways to bring dynamic and educational presentations in to the classroom.

The Checklist

1. Obviously, the first place to start would be with any school that you already have a connection. Perhaps a school that you or your children attended or where you know a teacher or administrator. Jog your memory and list any school-related connections you might have (teachers, librarians, administration, counselors, coaches, music/art specialists):

   _____

   _____

   _____

2. If you don't have any contacts at a school:
   - ☐ Visit the school district website and list schools whose students are in the age range of your market.
   - ☐ Visit each school's website individually and look for contact information for the media specialist or librarian. If you can't find the contact name or email, call the school and ask who handles the author visits.
   - ☐ Use the table on the next page to gather information.

3. Offer:
   - ☐ to send a copy of your speaker brochure
   - ☐ to share the link to your school program website page
   - ☐ details of your programs for the specific age groups
   - ☐ a copy of your book(s)
   - ☐ Lexile measurements and/or Accelerated Reader information, if applicable

4. Determine:
   - ☐ if your event will be in person or via video (and which platform)
   - ☐ if it will involve one or more group presentations
   - ☐ the duration of the visit
   - ☐ the number of students

- [ ] A/V availability and support (when Plan A doesn't work!)
- [ ] any specific requirements or restrictions

  ⏷ TIP: Find out ahead of time what the procedure for visiting the school entails in regard to security. In some states, you have to be pre-screened which may involve fingerprinting. For instance: Florida's Jessica Lunsford Act imposes background screening requirements on contractors who perform work on Florida public school property. The cost of the one-time screening is around $90. If you are unsure about the laws in your area, best to find out before you start trying to book school events.

5. Discussions about the money should involve:
- [ ] use of pre-order forms for book sales prior to the visit
- [ ] book sales on the day of the event
- [ ] speakers fee
- [ ] honorarium
- [ ] travel expenses if no speaking fee or honorarium
- [ ] any discounts that you offer to schools

  ⏷ TIP: Some authors use written contracts and others just spell everything out in the course of email exchanges. Make sure that the details (especially the ones involving finance) are in writing somewhere as reference to both parties.

School name	Contact and Title	Email	Phone

- [ ] **Way to be tenacious! Add this completed task to today's calendar!**

Task: SCHOOL EVENT
Category: Events

** Refer to School List on page 77

Once you have a contact at a school, it's time to work on getting a visit scheduled. This isn't the fun part, but working out all of the details ahead and being prepared will make the fun part even more fun. I promise.

The Checklist:
1. List the details of your upcoming event:
    - ☐ Date/Time of event: _____
    - ☐ School name: _____
    - ☐ Address: _____
    - ☐ Contact: _____
    - ☐ Contact email/phone: _____
    - ☐ Grades/ages: _____ # of sessions _____ # of students _____
    - ☐ Payment details: _____

    _____

    _____

    - ☐ Details of the proposed program: _____

    _____

    _____

    _____

2. Prior to your event:
    - ☐ Send discussion questions for those that purchase class copies.
    - ☐ Send book order forms (include backlist titles even if the program focuses on just one book). Forms should also include:
        - ☐ Author name.
        - ☐ Date of event.
        - ☐ Short paragraph about educational value of the event.
        - ☐ Book titles and prices.
        - ☐ Blank spaces for student's name and teacher's name.
        - ☐ Author website URL.

☐ Provide promotional, customized posters about your upcoming visit.

☐ TIP: If the school has a mascot, can you tie that into your presentation or your posters?

☐ If the event is a virtual visit (video chat), do a practice run with the school contact to make sure you both are able to use the platform with good audio and video connections. If you intend to add screen sharing or secondary videos or graphics, make sure you can do it without problems.

3. The day of the event:

☐ Know your audience - it is the students, not the educators!

☐ Roll with the punches. There may be glitches or challenges. It happens. Have a Plan B.

☐ Don't lecture. Present and perform.

☐ Have someone take pictures of you in action for use in future promotions. Don't photograph children unless you have permission ahead of time.

☐ **Going the distance! Add this completed task to today's calendar!**

Check off tasks once you add them to the calendars.

Tasks for SCHOOL Events	Schedule on calendar	#1	#2
Date of event	Date of event		
Confirm visit	1-2 weeks prior to event		
Send order forms	1-2 weeks prior to event		
Post-event tasks	1 day after event		

NOTES:

_____

_____

_____

_____

_____

Task: SPEAKING ENGAGEMENTS
Category: Events

Many speakers often publish a book to enhance their credibility as experts, increase revenue, or give them a takeaway item to further their brand. It can happen the other way around as well: authors can become recognized speakers, increase their credibility as experts in their field, and increase revenue. Although many authors find the prospect of speaking in front of an audience daunting, others have been able to overcome their fear and accelerate their careers.

Although non-fiction authors may seem to have the most obvious pathways to potential speaking topics, even fiction writers can speak on numerous topics of interest. In fact, that's a good place to get started…

The Checklist:

1. Make a list of potential topics that you feel comfortable talking about in front of an audience.

   TIP: Topics could include writing-related subjects or topics covered in your book.

   _____

   _____

   _____

   _____

2. Define potential audiences. These may or may not be the same groups you identified as your target book-buying audience previously. Think about where you might be able to find these groups.

   TIP: Start locally first. You probably have more contacts and a larger support system closer to home. Leverage any successful local speaking events into more opportunities regionally. Remember that many organizations will often contract program speakers six months or even a year ahead.

   Group _____

   Contact _____

   Group _____

   Contact _____

Group _____

      Contact _____

3. Ways to hone your skills:
   - ☐ Practice your presentation even before you have a speaking engagement lined up. Get comfortable with your message. Create a demo video as a sample of your ability. You can update it with clips from actual speaking events as you become more prolific as a speaker.
   - ☐ Speak in front of smaller groups like your writing or critique group.
   - ☐ Sign up for your local Toastmasters group.
   - ☐ Pay attention to speakers at conferences. Make notes about parts of their presentations you like or dislike.

4. Create a speaker's packet (page 132).
   - ☐ Include a description of your topics.
   - ☐ Add testimonials that you gather from your engagements.
   - ☐ Create an online version for your website.

5. When arranging a speaking engagement, confirm:
   - ☐ Date, time, location.
   - ☐ Topic of presentation.
   - ☐ Estimated attendance.
   - ☐ Speaking fees and what is covered (travel, lodging, food, etc.).
   - ☐ Payment method and schedule.
   - ☐ Room set-up and AV equipment provided.
   - ☐ Arrangement for book sales.

6. At the event:
   - ☐ Write your own bio for the person introducing you. This way you control the content.
   - ☐ Be prepared. Be early. Be gracious. Be yourself.
   - ☐ Have a cup of water handy - you don't want to be fidgeting with the lid on a water bottle in the middle of your speech.
   - ☐ Have a Plan B in case of technical difficulties.
   - ☐ Engage with the audience throughout your presentation.
   - ☐ Stay on topic and on time. Better to end early than to run over time and hold everybody hostage while you wrap it up.
   - ☐ Save some time for Q&A.

     TIP: Mention at the beginning of your presentation that you will save time for

Q&A at the end of your presentation so the audience will know that they can jot down questions ahead of time.

💡 TIP: Always repeat the question so everyone can hear it and understand your answer.

💡 TIP: Be prepared with a Plan B if no one asks any questions."Since no one has any questions, I'd like to end by sharing a personal story about ..." (something relevant to your speech).

☐ End with a call to action (Come buy my book, visit my website, follow me on Twitter, etc.).

☐ Offer a takeaway item with your contact information (outline of your speech, a coupon code for purchasing e-formats, SWAG, other marketing materials) so even if they don't buy your book at the end of the event, they can still find you later. Something of perceived value (resources list, etc.) will likely be saved longer.

☐ Announce where and for how long you will be selling and signing books at the conclusion of the event. This is an opportunity to sell not only the book related to the event but also any books from your backlist.

7. After the event:

☐ Send a hand-written thank you note to the organization or event coordinator.

☐ Ask for a testimonial or review.

☐ Look for social media photos on the organization's platforms that you can react to or share for extra exposure.

☐ **Making it happen! Add this completed task to today's calendar!**

Speaking engagement scheduling can be found below.

Check off tasks once you add them to the calendars.

Tasks for Speaking Engagements	Schedule on calendar	#1	#2	#3
Date of event	Date of event			
Press release	3 weeks prior to event			
Facebook Event page	2 weeks prior to event			
Email blast	1-2 weeks prior to event			
Post-event tasks	1 day after event			

TAKE A BREAK....

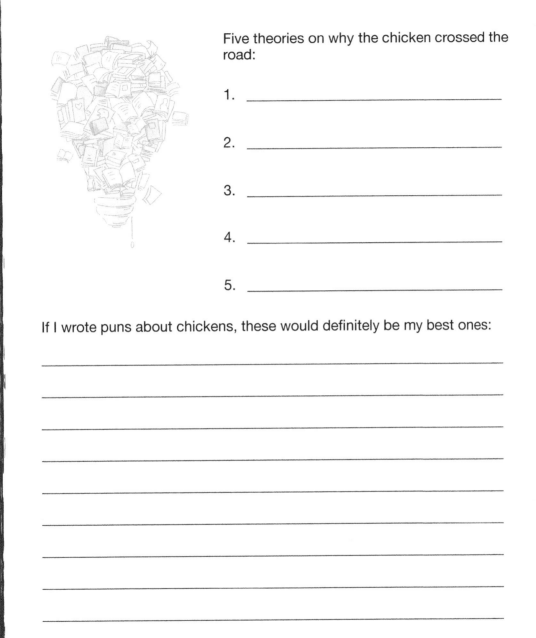

Five theories on why the chicken crossed the road:

1. _____

2. _____

3. _____

4. _____

5. _____

If I wrote puns about chickens, these would definitely be my best ones:

_____

_____

_____

_____

_____

_____

_____

_____

_____

#creativeweirdos #chickencrossing #mysterysolved

Task: BOOK CLUBS
Category: Events

The cornerstone of any indie author's success is their relationship with their readers and fans. One of the easiest ways to connect readers with authors is through book clubs (a group of people who read the same book title and then gather to discuss it). With all of the social media technology available now, speaking to a book club is a great resource for an indie author even if they are not geographically close.

Finding a Book Club:

1. Meetup.com is a great place to find book clubs in your area. There is no cost to create a meet-up profile if you don't have one already. *Book Clubs* is one of the popular categories.
2. There are a few websites that have listings of book clubs all over the world:
    1. http://www.readerscircle.org/
    2. https://www.my-bookclub.com
    3. Other: _____
3. Check to see if your local library has a bulletin board with book club information or ask the librarian.
4. Ask your local bookstore if they have book clubs that meet there.
5. Check with your community centers. Some YMCAs even have book clubs.
6. Goodreads has many online book clubs, sorted by genre, that you might be able to contact about your book especially if you are willing to participate in a Q&A with the readers via video chat.

Approaching a Book Club:

1. Research what sort of books the club reads, if possible, so that you know your book is a good fit.
2. Be polite and explain how you found them and give a very short synopsis of your book. Let them know you're available to do a personal appearance. Remember that sometimes books are scheduled months ahead of time and there may be a process that requires more than one person's suggestion.
    TIP: Offer a free book or portion of the book to the club organizer and a discount on the sales price for the members if possible.
3. When you do meet with the book club: offer swag, sign copies of your book, gently ask for reviews, pose for pictures, and gather email information for your list!

☐ **Way to go! Add this completed task to today's calendar !**

Task: ONLINE BOOK TOUR
Category: Events

The online book tour is also known as a *blog tour*. Traditionally an author would go from bookstore to bookstore selling books at each stop. With the internet, an author can now achieve the same effect by going from blog to blog! While book sales may not be immediate like they would be in person, a blog tour allows the author to widen their fanbase, get more recognized and practice answering interview questions. *Note: Most blog tours have a set duration. One or two weeks is just about perfect.*

How-to Steps:

1. Ideas for building your blog list:
   - ☐ Get recommendations from other authors you know.
   - ☐ Authors can hire companies to book blog tours for them. Pro: they have the contacts. Con: they don't know your book like you do and may not choose the best fitting blogs.
   - ☐ Do a Google search for <your book genre + blog + interview>

2. Ideas for fine-tuning your blog list (only pick the ones that meet your criteria):
   - ☐ Do they have any experience in blog tours?
   - ☐ Do they blog on a regular schedule?
   - ☐ Is it a good match for you and your brand?
   - ☐ Do they do author interviews?
   - ☐ Do they have a large following? If you can't find a number, how many followers do they have on other social platforms?

3. Preparing for a blog tour:
   - What do you feel more comfortable doing?
     - ☐ Guest post
     - ☐ Author printed interview
     - ☐ Exclusive content from book
     - ☐ A combination of them all!
   - Be prepared to send bloggers copies of your book to review. Make sure you understand their guidelines and time frames.
   - What else is in it for the blogger?
     - ☐ Expanded promotion of their blog to your social media contacts when you share the blog interview link.
     - ☐ Consider giving away prizes to their followers.

• Make sure to provide:
- ☐ Professional headshot
- ☐ Book cover image
- ☐ Author bio
- ☐ Contact information
- ☐ Buy links

• Your blogger list will grow organically over time as you discover new blogs. Keep updating this list so you have it for a reference when your next book comes out!

Blog URL	Contact	Email	# of Subscribers	Notes for Reference

☐ **You have what it takes! Add this completed task to today's calendar!**
Blog tour scheduling can be found below.

Check off tasks once you add them to the calendars.

Tasks for BOOK TOUR Event	Schedule on calendar	#1
Dates of event	Date of event	
Email blast	1-2 weeks prior to event	
Social media blast	1-2 days prior to event	
Post-event tasks	1 day after event	

Notes:

_____

_____

_____

_____

_____

_____

_____

_____

_____

_____

_____

_____

_____

General Marketing

**"Leverage the strength that you have:
that no one else can be you."**
Todd Wheatland

There are as many different ways to market as there are different books, and what works for one genre (or even one title) might not work for another. And here you thought the hard part was actually writing the book!

In the real world, as an independent author, you are in charge of your own marketing, but don't be overwhelmed. The basics of successful marketing are to start early, get educated, and remember that, at the heart of it all, marketing is about trust and relationships. These days it seems that everyone has a product to sell, and in such a noisy world, getting noticed and being heard isn't always easy. There are big complicated marketing campaigns you can design and implement, and there are many simple tasks that you can achieve that will make subtle but important differences. Both are necessary.

Task: EMAIL SIGNATURE
Category: Social Media / Email

Your *email signature* is the information attached at the bottom of your emails underneath the message. It is seen by anyone that opens your email which subtly increases your exposure in a low effort manner.

How-to Steps:
- In Gmail:
    1. Open your Gmail.
    2. In the top right, click Settings.
    3. In the Signature section, add your signature text in the box. If you want, you can format your message by adding an image or changing the text style.
    4. At the bottom of the page, click Save Changes.
- Don't have Gmail? Just google <add email signature + your email provider>

The Checklist:
Have you included:

☐ Name, Title, and Company (*ex: Patti Jefferson, CEO PJ Boox Bookstores*)
☐ A live link to your website (*ex: www.pjboox.com*)
☐ A live link Call to Action (*ex: Buy the book here!* with hidden Amazon link)
☐ Contact info - not email, of course! Phone, address if applicable.
☐ Social media links

> TIP: Pick only the platforms where you are active.

> TIP: Consider using linked icons for a cleaner look than actual links.

> TIP: Be smart about differentiating between professional and personal links.

Other things to consider including:
☐ Image such as logo or book cover

> TIP: Color is acceptable and adds pop in the midst of black text.

☐ Short single line editorial review
☐ Recent awards won
☐ Short quote (based on space availability and relevance)

☐ **Doing it like a pro! Add this completed task to today's calendar!**
☐ **Add to Calendar:** *Update in 3 / 6 / 9 months*

Task: SHIPPING AND PACKAGING

Category: General Marketing

Mail is just mail, right? Well, it doesn't have to be! Even shipping books can be an opportunity to expand your brand and promote your books. Remember that often the first impression that a reader/bookstore/venue has with you is the arrival of your books into their mailbox. We all know how important first impressions can be!

The Checklist:

☐ Media Mail: Use media mail whenever possible! A one pound package shipped via media mail costs less than $3 no matter where in the continental US you are shipping to or from. For reference, according to Amazon, the average book weighs less than a pound. Shipping more than one book? A package that weighs twenty pounds is still under $10.

  TIP: Weigh your book so you know what it costs ahead of time and can add it into your budget or your sales button.

- Media mail restrictions: You can only mail media (books, cds, dvd, cassettes, etc.). If you have swag to send, it needs to be sent separately.
- Media mail cannot contain advertising (so bookmarks, postcards, and flyers are out).
- Boxes shipped media mail are subject to inspection en route to their destination. If you are found in violation, the post office will assess the actual postal cost and bill either the sender or the recipient. Best to follow the rules!
- Shipping times can be two to ten days, but my personal experience is that it is only a few days.

☐ Shipping label: Think about your branding and create a return shipping label that has your logo, uses your colors, or even has a photo of the book cover.

☐ Packaging: Obviously, you want the books to arrive safely, but you also want to create a great first impression so be mindful of how you present your product.

  TIP: Wrap the book in tissue paper so it's like unwrapping a present!

  TIP: Use a printed sticker to hold the tissue paper. Add a call to action (i.e. Website URL or "Enjoy your book and don't forget to leave a review!")

  TIP: Use a rigid mailer (cardboard envelope) to safely ship your book.

  TIP: Books should fit tightly in your packaging to decrease the chances of covers and pages being damaged by shifting.

☐ **Outstanding! Add this completed task to today's calendar!**

Task: ELEVATOR PITCH
Category: General Marketing

Your elevator pitch should not be confused with a summary of the book (synopsis) or a back cover teaser (blurb). A pitch is a succinct and persuasive description of your book pared down to one or two sentences. The term comes from the idea that the summary of the book should be delivered in the same length of time as an elevator ride —usually less than a minute. You will need an elevator pitch when talking to book buyers, journalists, interviewers, or potential editors and agents.

The Checklist:
1. A sample of an elevator pitch might include:
   - ☐ The main character (and a characteristic that makes them unique)

   _____

   _____

   - ☐ The main conflict

   _____

   _____

   _____

   _____

   - ☐ What's at stake

   _____

   _____

   _____

   _____

2. Less than fifty words.
   💡 TIP: Don't mention other books. Remain unique!
3. Focus on the hook (i.e. the most important part of the book).
4. Edit/rewrite and then practice out loud until it sounds natural.

   _____

   _____

   _____

   _____

   _____

   _____

   _____

☐ **Yes! Another one done! Add this completed task to today's calendar!**
☐ *Repeat when/if you have a new title release.*

92

Task: ICE BREAKERS
Category: General Marketing

Not all authors, especially new ones, like to talk about themselves or even let people know that they have published a book. The whole idea behind an ice breaker is to get someone else, even a stranger, to start the conversation. By doing subtle *ice breaker marketing*, you seem approachable. Of course, if you are employing this sort of marketing, you should make sure to always have product with you to sell!

The Checklist:

1. Slogan ideas:
   - ☐ "I'm an Author. Ask me about my book!"
   - ☐ "I'm your next favorite author!"
   - ☐ "Indie Author"
   - ☐ "Authorpreneur"
   - ☐ "Google me. I'm kind of a big deal." *Be sure to include your name!*
2. Out-of-the-box options:
   - ☐ T-shirts - The nice thing about t-shirts is that they are pretty versatile in where you can wear them. *Cost $12 - $25*
   - ☐ Buttons - Make sure the button is large enough to read. Wear it or attach it to something that you wear every day (hat, coat, purse strap, etc.). *Cost $4 - $12*

     TIP: Instead of an author slogan, how about a quote from your book, a hook or even the cover. You can also use this as SWAG (page 130).
   - ☐ Table placard - A great choice for people who write or illustrate in public. *Cost $6 - $8*

     TIP: If you have a stack of books that need to be signed, why not do it at your local coffee shop while sipping a latte? People will be intrigued!
   - ☐ Luggage - I know an author who has vinyl lettering on her wheeled carry-on luggage so that when she is in the airport, she has a portable billboard! *Cost $20*
   - ☐ Mug - If you work in an office environment or have clients visit your non-writing job, a coffee mug - even an empty one - can be an advertisement for you. *Cost $12 - $16*
   - ☐ Calling cards - Go all out to get die-cut custom shapes for business cards. Make it book or logo related. If it's interesting enough, people will keep it longer and show it to their friends. *Cost $50 - $70*

☐ **Truly impressive! Add this completed task to today's calendar!**
If you can't order today, put a reminder on the calendar to order when you can.

Task: LIBRARY SALES
Category: General Marketing

Do libraries buy books? Yes, in fact, America's 123,000 libraries purchase nearly two billion dollars worth of books annually. That's a huge market! Do they buy books by indie authors? Well… some do but a lot don't. How do you find out which ones do and how do you get them to buy yours? It starts with some research…

The Checklist:

1. Determine which types of libraries are most likely to purchase your book:
   - ☐ Public library: serves cities and towns.
   - ☐ Academic library: serves universities and colleges.
   - ☐ School library: K - 12.
   - ☐ Specialty library: serves hospitals, military, corporations, etc.

2. You can find out some very basic information (name of branch, address, and phone number) of any public library by visiting www.publiclibraries.com. Choose your state and then your city to find them. Note: larger cities may have more than one location. Once you know the name of the branch(es) you are looking for, you can search the internet for their website for more information. Remember to check areas that you may travel to as well.

   _____

   _____

   _____

   _____

   _____

   _____

3. On the library's website, look for phrases like <Purchasing request for authors> or <Suggestion for purchase> and read the guidelines. Please note that libraries that do not buy indie books may still take donations which meet certain criteria. Some of the guidelines that libraries may require for purchase or donation include:
   - ☐ Publication date: _____
   - ☐ Publisher (Createspace is often not accepted): _____
   - ☐ Price: _____
   - ☐ ISBN (required): _____

94

- [ ] Intended audience: _____

- [ ] Binding type (Books must have a spine - spiral bound books are rarely acceptable): _____

- [ ] Ingram or Baker & Taylor distribution for easy ordering: _____

4. As with everything else in marketing, a personal connection is usually a better way to get your foot in the door. Here are some ideas on creating or cultivating those relationships:
   - [ ] Volunteer at the library for events.
   - [ ] Is the library participating in Indie Author Day in October? Or any other Indie author events?
   - [ ] Suggest a local author display with several other local authors.
   - [ ] Contact the *Friends of the Library* group for your library and get involved at that level. This might even lead to a speaking engagement if you have something to say.
   - [ ] Call ahead to schedule an appointment to speak with the Collection Development Librarian. Be prepared to have:
     - [ ] Book information listed above
     - [ ] References from booksellers that carry your book
     - [ ] Sales data
     - [ ] Any legitimate awards you have won for your book

5. Donating a book is always a way to get your book out there; however, it will probably not create a lot of sales in most instances. Most of the same rules above apply to book donations to the library.

   TIP: Consult your accountant for information on keeping records for donations.

Notes: _____

_____

_____

_____

- [ ] **You have what it takes! Add this completed task to today's calendar!**
- [ ] **Add to Calendar:** *Contact other libraries on the list in 3/ 6 / 9 months (or sooner!)*

Task: CONFERENCES
Category: General Marketing

Conferences are a great way to meet new people, educate yourself, and learn about resources that would be helpful to you in your book business. The most common format for a conference is a mixture of professional industry speakers, educational sessions, and networking opportunities. Some conferences also involve an opportunity to sell books. Determining what you are looking for in a conference is the first step.

The Checklist:

1. There is a difference in a writers conference and an author/publishing conference. Choose whichever works better for you. This task focuses on publishing conference but the same steps would apply if you choose differently. Use the list below to determine what you would like to get out of a conference and then we will look for something that suits your needs.
    - ☐ Book marketing techniques
    - ☐ Social media marketing
    - ☐ Pitching to TV or movies
    - ☐ Branding
    - ☐ Legal aspects of publishing
    - ☐ Record keeping and tax concerns
    - ☐ Foreign rights
    - ☐ Copyright challenges
    - ☐ Wholesale book distribution
    - ☐ Niche marketing
    - ☐ Networking
    - ☐ Other: _____
    - ☐ Other: _____
    - ☐ Other: _____

2. Specific areas of interest:
    - ☐ Specific genre: _____
    - ☐ Limited location area: _____
    - ☐ Special amenities in venue: _____

3. Find conferences in your area. Use the chart to write down information so you have a reference:
    - ☐ Google <your state + author conference>
    - ☐ shawguides.com
    - ☐ www.newpages.com/writer-resources

Conf. Name	Location	Website	Cost	Date	Registration deadline

4. What you will need at the conference:
   - ☐ Printed copy of agenda
   - ☐ Charged laptop/tablet (with cords) or notebook (in case there is no wifi)
   - ☐ Snacks (for sustenance, in case you get busy networking on a break and forget to eat lunch)
   - ☐ Bottled water
   - ☐ Business cards (for networking)
   - ☐ Sweater or jacket (hotel conference rooms' AC controls are unpredictable)
   - ☐ Cash (in case you want to buy a presenter's book or merchandise)
   - TIP: Network leading up to the conference and make appointments to speak one-on-one with speakers or vendors.

☐ **Congrats! Add this completed task to today's calendar!**
☐ **Add to Calendar:** *Conference dates and registration deadlines if attending.*

Task: QR CODES
Category: General Marketing

 You have seen them everywhere, but what are they really? And how can they help you market your book? A QR (quick response) code takes a piece of information from a 2D source (a manual, a restaurant menu, the back of your book, etc.) and makes selected content easily accessible for the user through a smart phone.

QR codes are more useful than standard barcodes because they can store (and digitally present) much more data, including URL links, videos, and/or text. The code above was one I used on the back of my first book, which was published in 2013. Even though the code is static, which means the link it directs to cannot be changed, you can still keep the information current and available by using domain forwarding or by changing content on the existing page.

The Checklist:
1. Ways to use a QR code:
   - ☐ Link to a specific page on your website.
   - ☐ Link to a video trailer on your YouTube channel.
   - ☐ Link to additional free content.
   - ☐ Add to your bookmarks for an exclusive offer.
   - ☐ On a poster at your book signing for a special reward.
   - ☐ Use different codes in different places to track responses.

2. How QR codes work:
   - Users have an app (free download) on their smart phones that scans the QR code similar to the way a scan gun reads a barcode at the checkout counter of a store.
   - The information that is read will automatically link the smart phone user to the destination linked to the barcode.
   - Smart marketers use very targeted destinations that complete a call to action (like a direct buy page) or an exclusive offer (like a free giveaway or contest).

3. Where to get a QR code:
   - ☐ There are many places to get a free QR code. Do a search for QR code makers.

- [ ] I use http://www.qr-code-generator.com/. It's easy to use for basics but also has the ability to upgrade to features such as campaign tracking, dynamic QR codes and multiple printing formats.
- [ ] Save your QR code in various formats for maximum flexibility of use.
- TIP: Make sure the destination page is optimized for mobile (otherwise the experience will be dismal and a waste of your marketing efforts and the user's time).
- TIP: Always test your code before you use it anywhere.
- TIP: Be sure to rename your file so you can find the correct code when you go to add it to your promotional materials. You will add it to your artwork just like any other graphic file.

4. I created this code exclusively for authors using this workbook. In order to see the special deal that is attached to it:
   - [ ] Go to the app store and get a QR code reader if you don't already have one on your phone.
   - [ ] Use the app to scan the code with your phone's camera which will take you to a hidden page on my website. I can update the exclusive offer for my readers as often as I like.
   - [ ] Enjoy!

Notes: _____

_____

_____

_____

_____

_____

- [ ] **That's what success looks like! Add this completed task to today's calendar!**

Task: BOOK TRAILER PLANNING
Category: General Marketing

The debate on whether or not a book trailer drives sales has been going on for years. While some people say that a book trailer infringes on the world that a book takes you to, others feel that the popularity of video in marketing makes a book trailer worth the expense and time. Done properly, a book trailer can offer the right amount of intrigue to have someone follow you on social media, visit your website, or sign up for your newsletter, even if they don't buy a book right away. Book trailers add rich content to your platforms and inspire sharing.

The Checklist:

1. Ideally, hire someone to do this professionally for you. If you can't fit it into your budget, there are ways to do it yourself.
   - ☐ The desired length of a book trailer should be no more than 60 - 90 seconds.
   - ☐ Plan out a script or storyboard of what you want to have happen BEFORE you start putting it together. Remember… a book trailer is meant to entice, NOT tell the book's whole story.
      - 💡 TIP: Use your synopsis as a guide to outline what sorts of images, clips, or music you want to use to convey the feel of the book. Searching for the right elements is time-consuming and planning what you need ahead will save you time.
   - ☐ Watch trailers from the authors you listed in your competition research task (page 15), as well as other authors in your genre. Get an idea of what inspires you and what you would like to avoid.
   - ☐ A slide show is not really a book trailer, but it is video content and very suitable for some social media advertising.
   - ☐ Keep branding, genre, and audience in mind when making your video.
   - ☐ Do not use licensed images, video clips, or music without proper permissions.

2. There are many resources online for license-free elements. Of course, photographers, videographers, and musicians deserve to be paid for their work, just like authors do, so don't rule out sites that require payment in order to find the perfect elements for your trailer. In some instances, donations are accepted so consider kicking in some money and love for other hard-working creatives.
   - Resources for license-free photos (use keyword searches):
      - ☐ unsplash.com
      - ☐ pexels.com

- [ ] pixabay.com
- Resources for license-free video clip (use keyword searches):
  - [ ] videoblocks.com ($99 one month subscription - cancel at anytime)
  - [ ] videvo.com (look out for sponsored content throughout the site which may have fees associated - attribution required)
  - [ ] pixabay.com
- Resources for license-free music:
  - [ ] imcompetech.com
  - [ ] freestockmusic.com (look out for sponsored content that is not free —unless you are willing to pay for music content)

3. Editing your trailer once you have all of the elements gathered will require some sort of editing software. Don't panic, it's not as hard as it sounds, and you may already have what you need (see page 32). Possible software includes:
   - [ ] For Macs: iMovie, Screenflow (free trial, purchase software), Wondershare Filmora (free download)
   - [ ] For PCs: Corel VideoStudio, Magix Movie Edit Touch (free), Wondershare Filmora (free download)

4. If your genre supports animation rather than video clips, here are some easy-to-use creation and editing programs:
   - [ ] Powerpoint (or Keynote for Macs)
   - [ ] Animoto (free trial period then monthly fee. Includes music tracks and tutorials)
   - [ ] prezi.com (similar to PowerPoint with free trial period and monthly fee upgrade)

Creating a book trailer is time-consuming and can be frustrating if you don't have any experience or are not tech savvy. Breaking this task down into smaller, more manageable pieces might make more sense if you are time-challenged and need extra time to educate yourself with tutorials. Add the small pieces to the calendar so you keep your momentum.
- [ ] Plan your trailer and outline (synopsis) and storyboard (1 hour)
- [ ] Search for appropriate video clips or images (2 hours)
- [ ] Search for music (1 hour)
- [ ] Choose and learn editing software (3+ hours)

- [ ] **You've got this! Add this completed task to today's calendar!**

Task: BOOK TRAILER PROMOTION

Category: General Marketing

If you are working with a professional on this task, be sure to verify that promotion is part of their service.

Congratulations on completing your book trailer! Now what?

The Checklist:

1. Upload your video to YouTube for starters (search for information on setting up a YouTube channel if you don't already have one).
   - ☐ Use keywords (what people might search for to find your book trailer)
   - ☐ Make sure your title and description are not confusing.

2. Other places to use your trailer to promote your book:
   - ☐ Add it to your website homepage.
   - ☐ Post it to your social media platforms. Remember video is easy to share and most platforms (like Facebook, Twitter, and LinkedIn) love video content.
   - ☐ Upload it to your Amazon Author page. Video content will add another layer of excitement to your book.
   - ☐ Goodreads is another platform that allows video content and gives you the ability to reach readers in a new way.
   - ☐ Add your trailer to your blog or make it available to a blogger who is interviewing you.
   - ☐ Play your book trailers on a tablet, computer, or even television screen during an author event to capture the attention of potential buyers and make them stay at your table longer.
   - ☐ Add a link to your latest trailer at the end of your last e-book to tease the reader with the next book in the series or a stand-alone in the same genre.
   - ☐ Send a link to potential book clubs. You will look professional, and your book will seem more compelling.
   - ☐ Add it to your email signature.
   - ☐ Send it to your email list and make a big deal out of it ("World Premier!").

   💡 TIP: Break this task up into smaller pieces. Add the small tasks to the calendar so you get your book trailer in as many places as possible for maximum exposure.

☐ **You're quite the hot shot! Add this completed task to today's calendar!**

Task: RETAILER LINKS
Category: General Marketing

By now, you probably have your books available in more places than just Amazon, but are you giving your readers that information? Adding information about other retailers who carry your books may increase your sales just by offering more options! It also lets people see that you are in demand.

The Checklist:

1. Use this list to organize the places that people can buy your books:
    - ☐ Online retailers (the usual sites, your publisher's website, smaller book-related sites, etc.): _____
    _____
    _____

    - ☐ Bookstores: _____
    _____
    _____

    - ☐ Specialty stores (gift shops, boutiques, museums, coffee shops, etc.): _____
    _____
    _____
    _____

    - ☐ Recurring events (farmers markets, monthly art nights, regular poetry slams):
    _____
    _____
    _____

TIP: Let the retailers that carry your book know that you have linked their venue to your website, and ask for a reciprocal link. It's basically free advertising for each of you. Win-win!

TIP: Use graphic icons as well as links on electronic media. Use icons on print media.

TIP: People will buy where you tell them to go. Where do you make the most money or get the greatest benefit from a sale?

☐ **Voila! You did it! Add this completed task to today's calendar!**

Task: GOOGLE ALERTS

Category: General Marketing

The world is large and, frankly, it's hard to keep track of it all. As an authorpreneur, you need to stay on top of what people are saying about you, your brand, and your products. You will want to share the good stuff with your fans and control the bad stuff so it doesn't become terrible stuff. So how do you find out when people are talking about you? Google alerts!

Step-by-Step:

1. Setting up a Google alert allows you to track a particular topic and have all of the information that bubbles up in the news automatically delivered to you. In this case, the topic of interest is you. You do NOT have to have a Google account to get Google alerts (but you DO need one for YouTube, Google+ and other platforms so you should have one anyway).
   - ☐ Go to: https://www.google.com/alerts.
   - ☐ Type your name in the Create an alert about… box.
   - ☐ Use the Show Options drop down menu to set up the parameters (how often to get the alerts, from what sources and where to deliver them).
   - ☐ Click the Create Alert button.
   - ☐ Add other varieties of interest to create other alerts: book titles, your publisher, topics of interest related to your book, etc.
   - ☐ You can edit your alerts at any time or stop the alerts altogether by simply deleting them.
   - ☐ You can set up as many different Google alerts as you want: track trends, your competition, your retailers, your book's subject, related topics, your market, etc.

2. Note: Yahoo Alerts work the same way, but you MUST have a Yahoo account in order to set alerts within their system.

3. If you choose to skip using the alerts and just occasionally Google yourself, here are some things to know:
   - ☐ Do it from a private window or incognito mode.
   - ☐ Pay attention to the first page as most users wont go farther than that.
   - ☐ Resist the urge to revisit negative results often as it may tell Google that there is more interest in that content than other results which may be positive.

☐ **Yippee, Skippy! Thats's done! Add this completed task to today's calendar!**
Update when you have new search topics.

TAKE A BREAK….

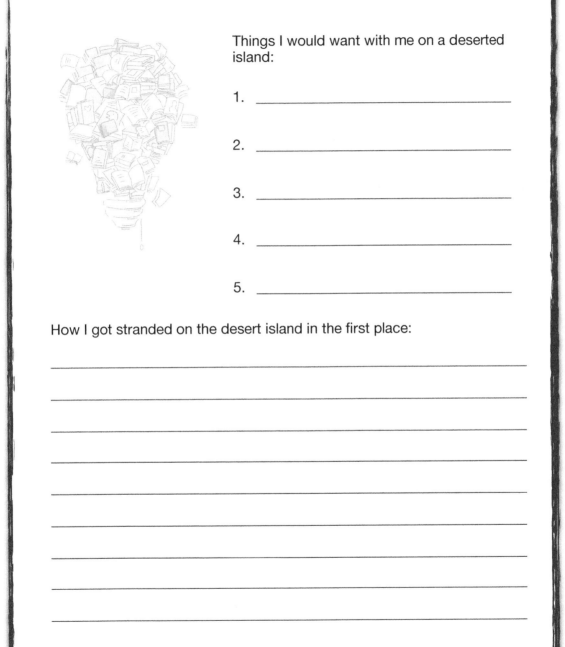

Things I would want with me on a deserted island:

1. _____

2. _____

3. _____

4. _____

5. _____

How I got stranded on the desert island in the first place:

_____

_____

_____

_____

_____

_____

_____

_____

_____

_____

#creativeweirdos #athreehourtour #coconutdiet

Task: HARO
Category: General Marketing

HARO stands for *Help A Reporter Out* and is an online database resource that puts journalists and bloggers together with credible sources in a variety of fields. HARO distributes tens of thousands journalist queries from highly respected media outlets each year (Alexa rankings of 1 million or less). So what does all this mean for an authorprenuer?

The Checklist:
1. As an author, you may be an expert on:
   - ☐ Writing
   - ☐ Publishing
   - ☐ Small business ownership
   - ☐ Public speaking
2. The subject of your book makes you an expert on:

   _____

   _____

   _____

3. As a blogger, you may need a source for:

   _____

   _____

   _____

   _____

Step-by-Step:
1. Go to www.helpareporter.com and sign up for the free subscription.

2. As a source, you will get up to three emails a day which will include dozens of queries from media sources.

   💡 TIP: The emails come at the same time each day: 5:45 am, 12:45 pm, and 5:45 pm EST every day. The earlier you can respond to relevant queries, the better your chances of being used as a source.

3. Find requests that you could legitimately add value to the conversation. Don't waste your time — or the reporter's — by pitching to irrelevant queries.

4. Submit your pitch:
   - TIP: Use HARO's system to pitch rather than your own email system. It will help keep the journalist organized and you will be able to see all of your past pitches easily in your HARO account.
   - ☐ Avoid generic subject lines. There will be competing sources, so be intriguing and unique.
   - ☐ Start with a personal greeting using the journalist's name.
   - ☐ Be succinct. Keep it to a few paragraphs, and don't be afraid to use bullet points. Journalists are busy people.
   - ☐ Answer questions.
   - ☐ Cite factual statistics to improve your credibility.
   - ☐ Stay on topic.
   - ☐ Edit your pitch. Typos or grammatical errors can kill your chances of getting the media opportunity.
   - ☐ Don't forget your website link. Your website should include your electronic media kit (page 38), which may contain extra information important to the news reporter.
   - ☐ Add a link to your Dropbox folder if you need to send high-resolution photos.

5. After your pitch has been sent:
   - ☐ Do not follow up with the reporter. If they mention you in their article, you will know! (see the *Google Alert* task on page 104)
   - ☐ If you do get a placement, share it on all of your social media and via email.
   - ☐ Send the journalist a thank-you note, mention the places that you shared it, and let them know you'd be happy to work with them in the future.

Notes: _____

_____

_____

_____

_____

☐ **You deserve a pat on the back! Add this completed task to today's calendar!**
Work checking HARO emails into your schedule as possible.

Task: BOOK AWARDS
Category: General Marketing

Do book awards really matter to indie authors? YES! Winning an award for your books gives your work validation, a chance at media attention, and may even increase your sales. Garnering a prestigious award may also aid you in finding an agent to represent you and your book. Best of all, you'll be able to market yourself as an award-winning author!

So how do you find the right awards for your book?

The Checklist:

☐ There are book awards for almost every genre. Search online for <your genre + book award>.

☐ Use the form to gather information. This will be a resource that you can use in the future as well.

☐ Do some research on the award:

    ☐ Who are the judges?

    ☐ What are the fees?

    ☐ What books have won in the past?

    ☐ Do the fees seem reasonable?

    ☐ What if you wish to enter the book in a second category? Are there discounts?

    ☐ What do the winners get? Medals? Awards dinner? Press releases? Prizes?

    ☐ Are there favorable reviews for the award?

    ☐ What is the publication date for entrants?

💡 TIP: Check to see if there are niche awards for your subject matter or for specific author attributes or affiliations.

💡 TIP: Come up with a plan for how to maximize a book award win. Have your media list together to send out a press release.

💡 TIP: https://selfpublishingadvice.org/allis-self-publishing-service-directory/award-and-contest-ratings-reviews/ is the link to the Alliance of Independent Authors. Not only do they provide a list of indie book awards, but they also provide a watch list of what to look for while seeking out a book award program.

Notes: _____

BOOK AWARD	GENRES	WEBSITE	COST	DEADLINE
FAPA President's Book Award	- 54 categories - Open to US authors	www.myfapa.org	$65 FAPA member disc.	May 31

_____

_____

_____

_____

_____

☐ **Whoop, whoop! Add this completed task to today's calendar!**
☐ **Add to Calendar:** _Add award deadlines to the calendar so you get your submissions done in time and budget for entry fees._

Task: PROFESSIONAL REVIEWS
Category: General Marketing

Reviews are a critical part of any author's marketing plan. With the ever-changing algorithms on social media, professional reviews are often more desirable than reader reviews. A critical assessment of your work by an established review company is perceived as more unbiased and can add visibility, as well as solidify your status as a respected author. The placement of such reviews is also a crucial part of the process.

The Checklist:

1. To find a professional review company that is right for your book, search online for <genre + review>.

2. Do some research on the review company. It can be very expensive, so you want to make informed choices.
    - ☐ What is the reputation of the review company?
    - ☐ What are the fees?
    - ☐ Is there a lower fee if you are willing to wait a bit longer for results?
    - ☐ What is the policy if your review isn't positive?
    - ☐ Where will the review be available?
    - ☐ What rights do you have for using the review?
    - ☐ What is the submission process?

3. The list on the next page is some of the larger, more established review companies. Your search will lead you to more options that may be more focused on your specific genre or subject matter, so add those to the blank list.

💡 TIP: Come up with a plan for how to maximize a positive review.
    - ☐ Have your media list together to send out a press release.
    - ☐ Consider adding your review to your printed marketing materials.
    - ☐ Leverage your review to get more exposure and events.

💡 TIP: Note that many professional reviewers want the manuscript months **before** a book release, so keep that in mind before the release of your next book, and add it to your production schedule.

4. Use the blank form on page 112 to gather information. Reference the *Online Book Tour* task (page 85) and google to find bloggers willing to review your book.

REVIEWER	GENRES	WEBSITE	COST	REACH
Booklist	Adult/Kid/ Audio/Video	www.booklistonline.com/get-reviewed	Free	80,000 print; 160,000 online
Kirkus	Adult/Kid	https://www.kirkusreviews.com/ indie-reviews/	$350+	3,000 print
Library Journal	Adult/Kid/ Audio, Video	http://www.libraryjournal.com/csp/ cms/sites/LJ/info/submissions.csp	Free	100,000
Book Life (Publishers Weekly)	Adult/Kid/ Audio	www.booklife.com	Free	25,000
School Library Journal	Kids/Audio/ Video	http://www.slj.com/about-us/ review-submissions/	Free	33,000 print; 44,000 online
Voices of Youth Advocates	Kid	http://www.voyamagazine.com/ submissions	Free	7,000
The NYTimes Book Review	Adult/Kid/ Audio	http://www.nytimes.com/ membercenter/faq/ books.html#booksqa2	Free	
The Horn Book		http://www.hbook.com/about-us/ submissions/	Free	13,000
Readers Favorite	All	www.readersfavorite.com/book-reviews.htm	Free (Express = $59)	
Self-Publishing Review	Adult	http:// www.selfpublishingreview.com/ get-reviewed/	$119 - $299	43K on social media
Indie Reader	All	https://indiereader.com/product/ indiereader-professional-review/	$225 (rush = $300)	
Indie BRAG	All Digital	https://www.bragmedallion.com/ submit-your-book/		
Blue Ink Review	All indie	www.blueinkreview.com	$395+	
Foreword Clarion	All indie	https://www.forewordreviews.com/	$499	

TIP: A good online resource for finding reviewers is The Indie View at http://www.theindieview.com/indie-reviewers/.

Other professional reviewers I found:

REVIEWER	GENRES	WEBSITE		REACH

Notes: _____

_____

_____

_____

_____

☐ **Excellent work! Add this completed task to today's calendar!**
☐ **Add to Calendar:** *Add submission deadlines to the calendar if you are planning to strategically space out reviews or need to budget.*

Task: READER REVIEWS
Category: General Marketing

Reader reviews are a crucial part of any successful indie book marketing. People often have a hard time being first to like or try something, but with someone else's recommendations, making the decision to experience the unknown becomes easier. With companies like TripAdvisor and Yelp, our society has slowly embraced the idea of leaving reviews for products and services. As an authorpreneur, it is vital to encourage readers to leave reviews that can then be leveraged for more followers and more sales.

The Checklist:
1. Where to leave reviews:
   - ☐ amazon.com or BN.com
   - ☐ Goodreads or other programs
   - ☐ Your website and/or publisher's website
   - ☐ Your Facebook author page

2. Where to ask for reviews:
   - ☐ On a page in the back of the book
   - ☐ On a postcard or bookmark
   - ☐ On your Facebook fan page
   - ☐ On other social media platforms
   - ☐ In private online messages
   - ☐ Via email using your readers list
   - ☐ Your street team.
   - TIP: Readers are more likely to leave reviews when they feel a personal connection. Asking for reviews should be like asking a friend for a favor.
   - TIP: Posting a reader's review to your social media occasionally will remind other readers that they should review your book as well.

3. How to leverage reviews:
   - ☐ Save copies of your reviews to be used on your social media, website, and marketing materials.
   - ☐ Add reviews to your media kit.
   - ☐ Add prepublication reviews to your book's front matter or back cover.

Ooh! Such a smarty pants! Add this completed task to today's calendar!

☐ **Add to Calendar:** *Ask for reviews at every other month. Leverage more often.*

Task: NEWSLETTERS
Category: General Marketing

You are an author and you write books. In order to market them, you also write social media content, website content, a blog, and, apparently, now you are supposed to be writing a newsletter! It sounds overwhelming, impossible, and even a bit unnecessary. It's not. A newsletter seems to be a much more personal communication with your readers and followers. They have given you permission to send information into their personal space (inbox). See the *Email list* task (page 44) for related information.

The Checklist:

1. Define the audience for your newsletter. This will dictate the content.

    ☉ TIP: Newsletters should be at least 75% informative or helpful to the audience and no more than 25% sales and promotion.

2. Popular formats for newsletters:
    - ☐ Curation - a collection of organic or culled newsworthy items.
    - ☐ Digest - short segments with direction to sources outside the newsletter.
    - ☐ Direct traffic to your website, social media or blog.
    - ☐ Single topic - create a repetitive theme such as: "Five Reasons for …" or "What you don't know about…"

    ☉ TIP: Keep your branding in mind. Can you play off your name, book series or tagline?

3. Possible elements for your newsletter:
    - ☐ Brief feature article
    - ☐ Bulleted statements of interest
    - ☐ Upcoming projects
    - ☐ Upcoming events
    - ☐ Contact information
    - ☐ Contests or promotions
    - ☐ Call to action

4. Establish a schedule that you can stick to, and also provide quality content. Consistency is key.

5. Select a mail platform. The two top contenders in this space are:
    - ☐ Mailchimp
    - ☐ Constant Contact

    ☉ TIP: Google <Mailchimp vs. Constant Contact> for the latest side-by-side comparisons to determine which one might be a better platform for you.

TIP: Templates will help you keep your newsletter in a consistent format and remind you to be brief.

TIP: The ability to track open rates and manage bounced emails in order to keep your email list accurate are invaluable.

TIP: Look for features that allow you to automate any part of the process. Be sure to go through the available training so you understand how best to use the platform and its features!

Notes: _____

_____

_____

_____

_____

_____

_____

_____

_____

_____

_____

_____

☐ **Woah! You're on fire! Add this completed task to today's calendar!**
☐ **Add to Calendar:** *At least once a month. Be consistent!*

Task: READING GROUP GUIDE

Category: General Marketing

Sales to groups such as book clubs or school groups are obviously important to authors because of the volume of books sold. As an added enticement to these sorts of groups, many authors create and promote Q&A, author interviews, and reading guides to serve as a way to start multi-reader conversations. A reading guide should allow the reader to engage with the book on a deeper level.

The Checklist:

1. Tips for getting started:

    TIP: Using the information that you gathered on page 17, check the questions other authors in your genre provide for their readers, and use their guides as a template for coming up with questions specific to your book.

    TIP: Using reader reviews of your book, look for questions or thoughts that seem to come up as possible themes for your reading guide.

    TIP: Google <author + reading + guide + templates> for more inspiration.

2. Elements:

    ☐ Introduction — short synopsis of the book.
    ☐ The story behind the story — the inspiration which led to the book
    ☐ Topics and questions for discussions.
    ☐ Supplemental resources — reference books or events that inspired your story, or use a call to action to drive traffic to other resources you have created (such as blog, newsletter, groups, etc.).
    ☐ Interview with the author — this can be a self-interview, a professional journalistic interview, or a collage of interview snippets from different sources.
    ☐ Author contact information — especially if you are available for video chatting with the group to answer questions in person.

3. Tips for writing guide questions:

    TIP: Do not ask yes or no questions. Dig deeper into characters, plot, themes, etc.
    Example: When Little Red Riding Hood entered the woods on her way to Grandma's house, she showed no fear. What do you think made her so brave?

TIP: Describe a key point in the story and then ask directly related questions.

> Example: In the story, the cow jumped over the moon and the little dog laughed to see such a sport. What do you think the dog was thinking and what effect did the cow's act ultimately have on the dish and the spoon?

TIP: Compare and contrast two characters within the book or characters with your readers.

> Example: Little Jack Horner was pleased with himself when he pulled a plum out of his pie. Describe a time when you were remarkably proud of yourself for your accomplishments.

TIP: Pose alternative actions or reactions.

> Example: Little Miss Muffet and the spider both seemed to enjoy sitting on tuffets, yet Miss Muffet was obviously frightened. What might have happened if Miss Muffet had stayed and gotten to know the spider better?

TIP: What is the biggest takeaway from the book?

> Example: What would you say was the greatest weakness of the two little pigs in their battle with the wolf who blew down their houses? How did the third little pig inspire them with his courage?

4. Places to put your guide:
   - ☐ Printed in the your back matter.
   - ☐ Downloadable from a website page (printable to share).
   - ☐ On your social media platforms as singular posts to start discussions.
   - ☐ On your street team Facebook group page to facilitate conversations.
   - ☐ Listed as "bonus material" in marketing to reviewers, bloggers, and for pitches.
   - ☐ As an incentive to sign up for your newsletter (exclusive content).

5. Make sure you have a professional review of any printed or electronic information before you share it with your readers.

Notes: _____

_____

_____

☐ **A gold star for you! Add this completed task to today's calendar!**
☐ **Add to Calendar:** *update in 6 months to add any new elements*

Task: BOOK DONATIONS
Category: General Marketing

There is irony in giving away books as a way to sell books, but if you are strategic in your donations, you can often gain exposure that may lead to more book sales. Using the information that you gathered about your target market, you can determine some of the best places to gift your book to increase word-of-mouth sales.

The Checklist:

☐ Review of your target audience:
   ☐ Your genre: _____
   ☐ Who is your target buyer: _____
   ☐ Where can you find them: _____
   ☐ What are their hobbies/jobs/organizations: _____
   _____

☐ Use the chart below to start thinking of places that make sense for you to donate your book. Add some of your own ideas.

X	Donations to:	X	Donations to:
	Hospital		Day care center
	Doctor's office		Homeless shelter
	Dentist's office		Prison
	School library		Car repair center
	Retirement home		Veterans organization
	Church		Disaster relief organization
	Community center		Friends of the Library
	Active duty military organization		Summer camp
	Other		Other
	Other		Other

☐ **Getting stuff done! Add this completed task to today's calendar!**
☐ **Add to Calendar:** *Add to calendar every few months if you discover new places to donate.*

Task: HOLIDAY MARKETING
Category: Marketing Materials

There are traditional holidays (like Easter or New Year's Eve) that are easily recognized and even more "Hallmark" holidays (like Mother's Day or Grandparent's Day) that we are aware of. Those dates, especially the gift-giving ones, may be easy to work into your marketing plan. There are, however, a million other "awareness holidays" that you can tie into promotional efforts, like National Ice Cream Day or Adopt-a-Pet Day.

How do you find these "holidays" ahead of time? And how can you leverage them even if they don't have any obvious tie-in to your book?

The Checklist:

☐ There are plenty of resources online for these types of holidays. Check out a few:
   ☐ www.timeanddate.com
   ☐ www.holidayinsights.com
   ☐ www.daysoftheyear.com
   ☐ TIP: Use the NOTES section of the calendars to write down dates that you want to use for promotional purposes. Brainstorm ways to use them.
☐ Look for ties to your genre, book title, characters, scenes, etc.
   ☐ TIP: Use special holidays in your prescheduled social media posts.
☐ Also pay attention to author, writer, and book holidays:
   ☐ January 18: Winnie the Pooh Day
   ☐ February 1 - 7: Children's Book Author and Illustrator Day
   ☐ February 14: Library Lover's Day
   ☐ March 2: Read Across America
   ☐ March 5: World Book Day
   ☐ April 28: Great Poetry Reading Day
   ☐ May: D.E.A.R. Month (Drop Everything and Read)
   ☐ July 30: Paperback Book Day
   ☐ October 12-18: Teen Read Week
   ☐ November 1: Author's Day
   ☐ Check the full list by googling <author + writer + book + holiday> or at www.ambassador-international.com/celebrate-books-year-36-literary-holidays

☐ **High five! Add this completed task to today's calendar!**
☐ **Add to Calendar:** *Use the NOTES section to write down the dates of pertinent holiday dates.*

Marketing Materials

"Creativity takes courage."
Henri Matisse

Remember the old saying, "You never get a second chance to make a first impression?" Well, that is definitely true when it comes to marketing your book. According to studies by psychologists at Princeton, the average consumer takes less than one second to form some sort of opinion about you, your products, or your brand. Less. Than. One. Second. Let that sink in for a minute.

Of course, it is important to make the right impression personally, but it is just as important to make sure your brand is making a good first impression even when you aren't physically present. Professional-looking marketing materials will help make the first impression of your brand a positive one.

Task: BOOKMARKS
Category: Marketing Materials

The most obvious piece of marketing material for authors would probably have to be bookmarks! It counts as SWAG because you give them away and also as a business card of sorts. Being very versatile, inexpensive, and possessing marketing longevity makes them a favorite of authors and readers alike.

The Checklist:

1. Ideas for bookmark content:
   - ☐ Author name
   - ☐ Author headshot
   - ☐ Website URL
   - ☐ Book covers
   - ☐ Social media icons
   - ☐ Author logo
   - ☐ QR code
   - ☐ Awards
   - ☐ Blurb

   💡 TIP: If you will be leaving them with booksellers, include distribution and ISBN information.

2. Design ideas:
   - ☐ One side or two? One-sided bookmarks leave you room to sign the other side for added value SWAG or for the reader to write notes. Two-sided bookmarks allow you room enough for multiple book covers and extended information.
   - ☐ The most common size is 2 x 8, although many other sizes are also used. For an extra cost, you can get rounded corners or even die-cuts in different shapes. If your book has a distinctive element, one of these specialty designs would definitely stand out.
   - ☐ As always, consider hiring a professional to do your graphics.
   - ☐ However, if you are going the DIY route, confirm with your print source that the size you want is an available option. Ask about additional costs to do two-sided, full color or bleed (where the design goes all the way to the edge of the trimmed bookmark).

   💡 TIP: If you have a scannable element, such a QR code, will the coating affect its use?

☐ In Canva,

    ☐ Select Use custom dimensions to create a blank template for your design. Choose px (pixels), mm (millimeter) or in (inches) to set your dimensions.

    ☐ Add a second page to design the second side if applicable.

    ☐ Remember your branding!

    ☐ Printers will ask for you send the design *head to head* which means top to top.

    ☐ When you are done, select to save as PDF - Print (Recommended) format with crop marks and bleed.

    ☐ Many online resources have easy templates you can use.

3. Selecting a printer:

    ☐ Contact a local printer who will work with you through your rookie mistakes.

    ☐ Use an online service such as VistaPrint ($200 for 250), GotPrint ($35 for 250) or PressGeek ($56 for 500) ** *Look for coupon codes to save money!* You will be able to upload your images directly to their website and order. Order a quantity that makes sense to you and keep in mind how often you may need to update them.

4. Samples of my personal bookmarks:

☐ **Well done! Add this complete task to today's calendar!**

Task: POSTCARDS
Category: Marketing Materials

Postcards are another versatile piece of marketing for authors. They can be used to announce new book releases to booksellers, promote events, or as direct mail pieces to your fanbase as an inexpensive reward. Utilizing both sides of the card can double the amount of information that you can share.

Standard sizes: 4" x 6" ■ 4.25" x 6" ■ 5" x 7" ■ 5.5" x 8.5" ■ 6" x 9"

The Checklist:

Uses for postcards:

1. To announce a new book release

☐ Add a photo of your new book cover to front with additional information about the book on the back.

💡 TIP: Because of the rectangular shape of a postcard, you can even make the front and back of the postcard look just like the front and back cover of your book (adding contact information, of course).

Note the use of :
☐ *headshot*
☐ *logo*
☐ *social media icons*
☐ *blurb*
☐ *website URL*
☐ *bulleted bio*

2. As an invitation to an author event

☐ Add a synopsis and new book cover to front with additional information about the book on the back.

💡 TIP: Leave blank space on the back to attach a sticker/label (Avery, etc.) with specific event information. You can run the labels through your home printer and only use as many as you may need.

Note the use of :
☐ *headshot*
☐ *synopsis*
☐ *social media icons*
☐ *website URL*
☐ *contact info*

3. To showcase an entire series

☐ Use the postcard to not only highlight a new book but also your backlist. *(Note: the dotted area on the sample shown is for visual clarification only and not actually printed on the card.)*

Note the use of :
☐ *headshot*
☐ *QR code*
☐ *social media icons*
☐ *website URL*
☐ *branding elements*

4. As a direct mail piece

☐ Create a postcard that can actually be sent through the mail. Ask your printer for a template so that you are following USPS rules.

Note the use of :
☐ *synopsis*
☐ *contact info*
☐ *website URL*
☐ *branding elements*

5. Other uses

☐ Swag: Consider making your postcards collectible and using them as giveaways to fans at events.

☐ Handouts for booksellers at checkout: this type of postcard might feature something newsworthy such as a new book award win or an exceptional review.

☐ Rewards for street team: custom postcards are a nice way to say "thank you" for all they do for you.

TIP: For more information on postage options and direct mail solutions, visit the USPS guidelines at www.usps.com/business/advertise-with-mail.htm .

TIP: Canva has a size template for postcards which is very user-friendly.

TIP: Contact your local printer, Vistaprint (50 = $10+), GotPrint (100 = $26+) or other online printers for pricing.

☐ **Hats off to you! Add this completed task to today's calendar!**

Task: BANNERS
Category: Marketing Materials

Banners are one of the most common visual elements used for marketing and promotional purposes, so if you are doing author events, you might want to consider getting a banner to help draw attention to your table or tent. The type of banner you need will depend on the types of events you attend. Outdoor events need banners that will withstand the elements, including sun, rain, and especially wind. Banners for indoor events will likely need to be free standing.

The Checklist:

1. Types of banners:
   - ☐ Vinyl banners are probably what you think of first when you think banners. They come in a wide variety of sizes and often come with grommets so they can be hung between canopy supports or other vertical spaces. These banners are usually UV and water-resistant.
     - • Pros: fold up flat for storage, very durable, fairly inexpensive
     - • Cons: need additional elements to display (bungee cords or string), difficult to attach to solid vertical spaces
   - ☐ Retractable banners are becoming increasingly popular at indoor events. Their sleek design allows for convenient storage within the base. They come in a wide variety of sizes including a tabletop version.
     - • Pros: easy to transport and set up
     - • Cons: can be top-heavy and, thus, unstable

2. Tips for designing your banner:
   - 💡 TIP: Use author information instead of book information to keep from replacing your banner with each new book release.
   - 💡 TIP: If you do have a series, consider the clothesline approach: small vinyl banner of each book cover hung from one line. It makes it easy to add more titles in the future.

3. Pricing examples:
   - • Retractable banners: Vistaprint ($83), BannersontheCheap.com ($72), and Signs.com ($104)
   - • Vinyl banners: Vistaprint ($32), BannersontheCheap.com ($25), and Signs.com ($36)

☐ **You are the top banana! Add this completed task to today's calendar!**

Task: BOOKPLATES
Category: Marketing Materials

Bookplates have been around for centuries with very few changes. Traditionally, a book plate is a decorative label stuck in the front of a book, bearing the name of the book's owner. So how can indie authors use bookplates to market their books? In today's world of print-on-demand (POD) book sales, there are many scenarios where a reader may get a book that was shipped directly from a POD source like Createspace or Ingram Spark rather than the author directly. In that case, the opportunities for the coveted author signature don't exist. It boils down to a choice of paying for shipping twice or sending a signed version of a bookplate separately for just the cost of a stamp.

The Checklist:
1. Art-centric online markets (such as Etsy or Zazzle) are good sources for finding pre-made and unique custom bookplates.

    TIP: Choose a blank design that will give you space to write a personal note to your fans.
2. Vistaprint and other online design and print websites also have options for stickers that can be used as bookplates.
3. DIY bookplates can be designed on Canva using the *custom dimensions* option. If you are printing your own, find the proper label size first and then create the design accordingly. Avery #8168 (3.5" x 5") is a great size and at $13x for 100 labels, it's a great deal as well!

    TIP: Custom bookplates make great rewards for your street team or SWAG as a giveaway to fans.

    TIP: In your book, offer signed bookplates to your readers via a link to your website. This will drive traffic to your site, gather reader info and gain a personal touch with readers you might not know about otherwise.

☐ **Super amazing! Add this completed task to today's calendar!**

Task: POSTERS

Category: Marketing Materials

Posters were used to advertise the plays of Shakespeare in the 1500s and reached mass production in 1796 when German actor and playwright, Alois Senefelder, invented the process of lithography. How has something that has been around for centuries stayed so relevant in today's marketing world? Simple… posters serve as a semi-permanent option for grabbing attention from a broad audience. They make a strong visual impression that lingers in the consumer's mind while not breaking the piggy bank.

The Checklist:

1. Ways to use posters to promote:
   - ☐ Using your audience profile, put posters up in areas where your target market is likely to see them.
   - ☐ Place posters in venues to announce an upcoming author event.
   - ☐ Check with venues that stock your book to see if they have room for non-event, promotional posters.
   - ☐ Offer them to your street team for distribution or as a reward.
   - ☐ Depending on the quality of your poster, you may consider offering it for sale on your website as an ancillary product.

2. Elements to consider for your poster:
   - ☐ Author headshot
   - ☐ Book cover
   - ☐ Excerpt from a review
   - ☐ Branding elements: logo, elements and tagline
   - ☐ Website URL
   - ☐ Social media icon
   - ☐ QR code
   - ☐ Awards
   - ☐ Blurb

3. Ideas for your poster:
   - ☐ Inquire at the venue about space availability and quantity.
   - ☐ Create various sizes for display flexibility.
   - ☐ Laminate for longevity if you plan to reuse them.
   - 💡 TIP: For author events, create your poster with blank space so you can add specific information for each event and add versatility to your design.

💡 TIP: Given the popularity of memes on social media, consider a quote from your book as the primary visual element of your poster.

4. Resources for posters:
   ☐ Your local independent printer
   ☐ Business supply stores like Staples ($10 - $36)
   ☐ Online printing companies like Vistaprint ($9-$32) and GotPrint (minimum quantity is 100)

   💡 TIP: Make sure you have someone else double-check your poster for typos and other errors. In most cases (especially online), printers will not double check your content.

EVENT POSTER SAMPLE

1. Author logo
2. Social media icons
3. Professional headshot
4. Date and time (I can put a strip over this part with a new date and time to reuse the poster)
5. An award for one of my books
6. The cover of the book I was featuring for the event (close to Valentine's Day, so the book with the love theme)
7. The address of the venue (in case the poster is displayed somewhere other than the venue)
8. My website URL
9. My backlist, (which would also be available at the venue on the day of the event)

☐ **Cool beans! Add this completed task to today's calendar!**

Task: SWAG
Category: Marketing Materials

I have often heard that the term swag is an acronym for Stuff We All Give Away (or Stuff We All Get) but it is actually from a derivation of an English term for "loot" popular in the 17th century. Regardless of where the term originated, its understanding in today's vernacular is that of free stuff given away as a reward and for marketing purposes. Note: Swag that works for one author might not work for another so figuring out what will work for you isn't always easy.

The Checklist:

1. Things to consider when choosing swag:
   - ☐ Who is your target audience? What sort of giveaway items might appeal to them?
   - ☐ Is it easy to ship if you are using it for a giveaway?
   - ☐ Is it easy to transport if you are traveling?
   - ☐ Can it be branded?
   - ☐ What is its shelf life? Will people who get it keep it around?
   - ☐ Can your swag also double as marketing material?
   - ☐ What is your budget and your return on investment (ROI)?

2. Depending on the items, some things are best deemed merchandise and sold for at least cost rather than handed out Mardi Gras parade style to everyone who passes by.

3. Some items favored by authors as swag:
   - ☐ Bookmarks (cheap to hand out in bulk, easy to mail, long shelf life)
   - ☐ Stickers and temporary tattoos (excellent option for children - also coloring pages)
   - ☐ Pens (a popular necessity, challenging to ship flat, inexpensive to giveaway)
   - ☐ Rubber bracelets (collectible, long shelf life, lightweight, and easy to ship)
   - ☐ Buttons (easy to get with your book covers or a quote from your book)

4. Where to find the coolest swag:
   - ☐ Etsy and other art-centric sites offer unique items to help you stand out
   - ☐ Stickermule.com for stickers, decals, and buttons
   - ☐ Specialty and promotional companies (I use www.garrettspecialties.com)
   - ☐ Google search for specific items

What are you waiting for? Order some swag!

☐ **Hip hip hooray! Add this completed task to today's calendar!**

Task: BUSINESS CARD
Category: Marketing Materials

Nothing is more old-school for marketing a business than a business card, but being prepared when someone asks "What do you do?" might earn you a new reader or even a new street team member! The low cost and small size of business cards make them easy to keep on hand.

The Checklist:

1. Elements to consider for your business card:
   - ☐ Author headshot
   - ☐ Book cover
   - ☐ Branding elements: logo, elements and tagline
   - ☐ Website URL
   - ☐ Social media icons
   - ☐ QR code
   - ☐ Contact information
   - TIP: leave off any information which isn't vital.

2. Ideas for your business card:
   - ☐ Use both sides
   - ☐ Don't use a font size that requires a magnifying glass
   - TIP: Gotprint.com offers some special shapes for cards such as circles, ovals and squares to add a bit of WOW factor ($30)

3. Resources for business cards:
   - ☐ Use Canva and design your own.
   - ☐ Have a graphic designer lay out the cards for you.
   - ☐ Order them from your local independent printer.
   - ☐ Order from business supply stores like Staples.
   - ☐ Order from online printing companies like Vistaprint.
   - TIP: Don't buy 1,000 cards if it will take you a long time to use them up. You may want to update when a new book is released or when you add a social media platform.

☐ **No excuses! Add this completed task to today's calendar!**

Task: SPEAKER PACKET
Category: General Marketing

Public speaking and back-of-the-room sales can be a substantial source of income for authors. Creating a speaker packet is an important tool to have available as you plan speaking engagements (page 80) as it lets people know your qualifications, topics, and pricing all in one flyer or brochure.

The Checklist:
You may need two versions of the speaker packet: a physical copy to mail (or hand out in person or via street team) and a digital version for easy access online.

1. Information needed for both physical and digital versions:
   - ☐ Introduction
   - ☐ Name
   - ☐ Expertise/Qualifications
   - ☐ Applicable awards
   - ☐ List of topics (use chart below)

Topic	Who is the audience?	Description (value to audience?)	Duration of presentation?	AV requirements

- ☐ Endorsements
- ☐ Speaking fees (some authors include them, others just give contact information to get custom pricing)
  - ☐ TIP: Check other authors' speaking fees if you are just starting out. Adjust accordingly for your lack of experience.
- ☐ Discount availability
- ☐ Contact information
- ☐ Talking points for interviewers
- ☐ Professional photos: author, book covers, previous speaking engagements
- ☐ List of audio/visual setup and requirements
- ☐ Sample pre-order form

2. Additional information needed for digital versions:
   - ☐ Video samples of previous speaking engagements
   - ☐ Calendar of upcoming and past events
   - ☐ Downloadable pre-order form (.pdf file)
     - ☐ TIP: Design order forms to fit two per page, and write in the third person

3. Website (digital version)
   - ☐ Create a separate page for your speaker information.
     - ☐ TIP: Keep the calendar, testimonials, and all other information updated.

4. Printed (physical version)
   - ☐ Add a link to your YouTube channel or website for video samples of your presentations.
     - ☐ TIP: Print in short runs to keep information current.
     - ☐ TIP: If you have multiple pages or additional marketing materials, use a branded folder with pockets.
     - ☐ TIP: Consider creating a dvd of some of your speaking events to include in the packet.

NOTES: _____

_____

_____

☐ **Thumbs up! Add this completed task to today's calendar!**
☐ **Add to Calendar:** 6 month update

Networking

**"If you want to go fast, go alone.
If you want to go far, go with others."**
African Proverb

There are many forms of networking and almost all of them are important to the independent author. Whether it is networking to find other authors for critiques and moral support, creating a street team from network connections, or chatting with groups of potential readers, the smart indie author realizes that while writing can be isolating, promoting your book doesn't have to be.

The key point to successful networking is understanding that people are much more likely to do business with you if they know, like, and trust you. Networking gives you the opportunity to present yourself and your work in a personal way, and build strategic relationships. Done genuinely, you can convert prospective readers into buyers who will not only support you with sales, but also be a strong force in your word-of-mouth marketing. Even the most introverted author needs to master the art of networking.

Task: PROFESSIONAL ORGANIZATIONS

Category: Networking

Whether you are looking to hone your craft, stay up-to-date with the latest industry trends, or just network with your literary peers, professional writing and publishing organizations offer a single authorpreneur a chance to be part of a collective voice.

The Checklist:

1. Reasons to join a professional organization:
   - ☐ Provides credibility to your position as an author/publisher
   - ☐ Networking with others on the same career path
   - ☐ Continued informational growth

2. Do a key word internet search for:
   - ☐ <author+professional+organization+your genre> to find groups that focus on your genre (i.e. Romance Writers of America)
   - ☐ <author+professional+organization+your state> to find groups whose members are geographically centered (i.e. Florida Authors and Publishers Association)

3. Determine what benefits you are looking for in an organization:
   - ☐ Smaller regional chapters _____
   - ☐ Awards _____
   - ☐ Newsletter _____
   - ☐ Marketing advice _____
   - ☐ Educational workshops _____
   - ☐ Conferences _____
   - ☐ Online resources _____
   - ☐ Networking _____
   - ☐ Discounts on industry services _____
   - ☐ Insurance _____
   - ☐ Other _____

4. Using the chart on the next page, gather information about organizations that may be useful to you in growing your book business.

   TIP: Membership dues to professional organizations may be tax deductible. Please consult your accountant for financial and tax advice.

Organization	URL	Reg. Chap.?	Benefits	Dues
The Authors Guild	www.authorsguild.org		Publishing industry updates & advice; marketing/social media advice; website building & hosting, medical	$100 - $125
The Alliance of Independent Authors	www.allianceindependentauthors.org	No	Advice forum, handbooks & guides, discounts, affiliate program	$99 - $599
Society of Children's Book Writers and Illustrators	www.scbwi.org	Yes	*The Book: The Essential Guide to Publishing For Children*, grants, podcasts	$95
Romance Writers of America	www.rwa.org	Yes	writer's toolkit, critique partner match-up, conference	$99

☐ **Aren't you the clever one! Add this completed task to today's calendar!**

Task: SOCIAL MEDIA NETWORKS

Category: Networking

The key component to social media is the "social" part. There are countless author groups on Facebook and, in general, each of them have a focus on a specific area of the independent author industry. Many of them have to do with marketing and promotion.

The Checklist:

1. **AUTHORS'** groups online:
   - Determine what sort of author-to-author networking you are looking for:
     - ☐ Moral support and motivation _____
     - ☐ Industry information sharing _____
     - ☐ Promotion and marketing tips _____
     - ☐ Critique group _____
     - ☐ Review exchange _____

   - How to find worthwhile author/writer groups on social media platforms:
     - ☐ Get recommendations from other authors.
     - ☐ Do a platform search for <author+ writer+ type of group from list above>
     - ☐ Read the details of the group to see if it seems useful to you.
     - ☐ Lurk for a few days after joining to get a feeling for the group and how it flows before making your own posts.
     - ☐ If you decide to stay in the group, be sure to contribute to the conversation. Author groups should be two-way streets and beneficial for all.

     💡 TIP: If you belong to a professional organization, check to see if they also have a "members only" forum group online. These have become very popular and are often listed as a benefit of membership.

2. **READERS'** groups online:
   - Determine what sort of reader networking you are looking for:
     - ☐ Promotion of your work _____
     - ☐ Find ARC (Advanced Readers Copy) readers _____
     - ☐ Feedback from potential readers _____
     - ☐ Study genre trends with actual readers _____

   - How to find worthwhile reader groups on social media platforms:
     - ☐ Get recommendations from other authors in the same genre.
     - ☐ Do a Facebook search for <your genre + readers>

- [ ] Read the *About* details of the group to see if it seems to be useful to you.
- [ ] Lurk for a few days after joining to get a feeling for the group and how it flows before making your own posts.
- [ ] If you decide to stay in the group, be sure to contribute to the conversation. As an author of the genre, you should also be a reader of the genre.
- [ ] Don't be spammy!

3. Can't find what you are looking for? You can create your own group on Facebook!
   - [ ] Decide on the who, what, and why of your group _____

_____

- [ ] Use the pull-down menu at the top right of your Facebook page to create a new group. Select Create Group.
   - [ ] Name your group: choose something that clearly defines the group.
   - [ ] Add some people: just add a close friend or family member so that Facebook lets you finish the set-up process. Let other potential group members make their own decisions to join your group once you are ready to get started.
   - [ ] Select privacy settings: Your choices are:
     • Public: anyone can find the group and anyone can join it
     • Closed: anyone can find it, but they must be approved by you (or another administrator)
     • Secret: it doesn't show up in searches, and members must be approved
   - [ ] You can create questions which help you determine a potential member's eligibility for inclusion.

TIP: Life is too short to stay involved with any group that isn't serving some sort of purpose for you. Don't be afraid to leave and search for different groups with better engagement.

TIP: LinkedIn is an excellent platform to find professional authors for networking.

TIP: Goodreads is a platform designed for its members to create specific groups, including authors. So not only is it a vehicle for readers to share and authors to promote, but it is a way for like-minded people to network.

- [ ] **You're brilliant! Add this completed task to today's calendar!**
- [ ] **Add to Calendar:** *Add groups as you have time/need or once a month.*

Task: AUTHORS' GROUPS

Category: Networking

You may already belong to online author groups or forums (page 139) but if you have the opportunity to engage with other authors in person, grab it! Of course, most authors have limited time for extra-curricular activities such as social engagements for the sake of work, so how do you find and focus on the most beneficial groups for you?

The Checklist:

Note: See page 144 for ideas on starting an author group yourself if you can't find an existing local or regional group of writers where you live!

1. Determine what sort of author-to-author networking you are looking for:
    - ☐ Moral support and motivation _____
    - ☐ Industry information sharing _____
    - ☐ Promotion and marketing tip _____
    - ☐ Inspirational speakers _____
    - ☐ Review exchange _____
    - ☐ Critique group _____
2. Use Google search tools to search for <author + writer + group + city>.
3. Check to see if a professional group that you belong to has regional chapters in your area. If not, inquire about how to start one.
4. Ask other local authors for recommendations.
5. Start networking!

Group	URL	# Members	Purpose

- ☐ **Sensational! Add this completed task to today's calendar!**
- ☐ Add to Calendar: *add meeting dates to the calendar so you don't forget to attend.*

TAKE A BREAK….

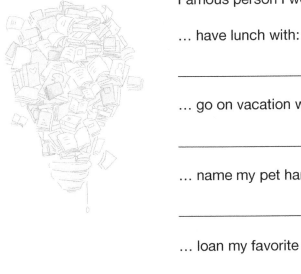

Famous person I would like to…

… have lunch with:

_____

… go on vacation with:

_____

… name my pet hamster after:

_____

… loan my favorite sweater to:

_____

When I am famous, things I will do for the "little people"…

1. _____

2. _____

3. _____

When I am famous, things I will not do…

1. _____

2. _____

3. _____

#creativeweirdos #sandwicheswithbobdylan #wheniamfamous

Task: CHARITY PARTNERSHIP
Category: Networking

Aligning yourself with a charity is a great way to get more exposure as an author as well as help your community by giving back. Because relationships are such an important component to your marketing plan, getting involved with a cause can be a win for all parties involved.

The Checklist:
1. Brainstorming to find the right charity partnership:
   - ☐ Personal connection: _____
   - ☐ Charity you volunteer with: _____
   - ☐ Local charity: _____
   - ☐ Search <charity + city> _____
   - ☐ Tie-in with character or plot of your book: _____
   _____

   - ☐ Add tie-in to keyword search (ex. Add character profession like <fireman> or plot focus like <bullying> _____
   _____
   _____

   - ☐ Tie-in with literacy: _____
   Search <charity +Literacy> and then narrow by genre if necessary.

   💡 TIP: Check out the charity and its specifics on www.Charitynavigator.org to ensure that your brand and their philosophies are in line.

2. How to get started:
   • Use the chart on the next page to gather information about possible charity partners.
   • How you can help them:
   - ☐ Donate a portion of profits during a certain time period _____
   _____
   - ☐ Participate in their events _____
   _____
   - ☐ Do joint marketing for the cause _____
   _____
   - ☐ Social media campaigns _____

☐ Contact the charity to talk about a possible collaboration.

💡 TIP: Add any charitable involvement to your press kit with contact info.

💡 TIP: If you are aligned with a specific charity for an indefinite period of time, make it a prominent part of the marketing plan:
- ☐ Social media platforms
- ☐ Email signature
- ☐ Book jacket or blurb

CHARITY	URL	CONTACT	WHO BENEFITS	WHAT CAN I DO TO HELP?

☐ **Marvelous! Add this completed task to today's calendar!**
☐ **Add to Calendar:** *Keep an eye out for other charitable opportunities that make sense for you to be involved with.*

Task: MEETUP
Category: Networking

Meetup is a social platform that helps people find groups with similar interests, backgrounds, or goals. Sorted geographically, you can find people who celebrate a certain nationality, gather for the shared love of a sport, or just wish to hang out with others to support a worthwhile cause. Face-to-face interaction can be a rewarding way to not only get educated in your business, but also help you build your street team and fanbase.

The Checklist:
1. How to use Meetup:
   - ☐ Go to www.meetup.com and sign up for free.
   - ☐ Search for existing author or writer groups in your desired area.
   - ☐ Change the miles you are willing to travel to participate into the required field if you want to widen your search.
   - ☐ Determine what you are looking for in a group:
      - ☐ critiques
      - ☐ marketing tips
      - ☐ writing techniques
      - ☐ social interaction
      - ☐ education
   - ☐ When you find a group, read their purpose and check out their information. Joining a group does not obligate you to participate and you can always ask the group coordinator questions for clarity.

2. If you can't find a group, you can always create one of your own. Things to consider about your Meetup group:
   - ☐ Clearly define the group and its purpose:

   _____

   _____

   - ☐ Who should join and why:

   _____

   _____

   - ☐ Create a schedule for events and meeting dates and times:

   _____

   _____

   - ☐ Determine the size for the group: _____

☐ Outline any areas of concern, and state the rules of the group:

_____

_____

☐ Look for similar skill/experience levels (unless this is a class situation):

_____

_____

☐ Realistic expectations/goals: _____

_____

3. How to set up your own Meetup group:
   ☐ Setting up your own group is a pretty simple process. There are tutorials within the app/program to help you with scheduling, group setting, membership maintenance, financials, and even tips for finding sponsors to support your group. The following are fields that are required to set up your own Meetup group (refer to your notes above):
      ☐ What will your Meetup be about? There are lists of options and you can pick all that apply.
      ☐ What will the group be called? Be specific more than clever. You want potential members to be able to find you.
      ☐ Have a concise group description. You want to be clear about what the group has to offer its participants. This field requires at least 50 characters so you have room to expound on details.
      ☐ Fees: While signing up for Meetup is free, there is a cost to creating and running your own group.
         • Basic plan = $9.99 per month: can create up to three groups and up to fifty members per group
         • Unlimited plan = $14.99 per month: no limit to number of groups and no limit to number of participants in groups
   ☐ Your group must be approved before it officially launches.
   ☐ New groups are announced directly to Meetup members in the area based on interests listed in their profiles.

4. Meetup is also a good way to find possible target audiences by offering sponsorships to them. Ways to sponsor a group include:
   ☐ Cover the group's subscription fee
   ☐ Offer a discount to your product
   ☐ Donate meeting space
   ☐ TIP: Post a flyer about your Meetup group at your local coffee shop or library as well as on your social media platforms.

☐ **Nothing short of stellar! Add this completed task to today's calendar!**

Task: GUEST BLOG
Category: Networking

What & Why:
While it may be important to create and maximize your own blog, it can be just as beneficial to guest blog in someone else's space. If you submit well-written, fresh content for a successful blog, you can open the door for discovery by a new audience and increase your base as well as your sales.

The Checklist:
1. Reasons to incorporate guest blogging into your marketing strategy:
   - [ ] Establish new connections.
   - [ ] Gain recognition as an expert in your field.
   - [ ] Create a call to action to build your list.
   - [ ] One click from new sales.
   - [ ] Elevate your SEO (Search Engine Optimization) with click-through options to your blog or website.

2. How to find blogs that welcome guest bloggers:
   - [ ] Get recommendations from authors that you know who guest blog.
   - [ ] Google <guest+blogs+posts+authors>.
   - TIP: Look for blogs that consistently have multiple comments at the end of the article. Knowing that a blog gets great engagement makes doing a guest blog more worthwhile.
   - TIP: Don't just approach book or literary blogs. Focus on the niche markets that may be interested in you and your books. Google <top+blogs+about+<your niche>.

3. How to pitch for a guest blog spot:
   - [ ] Be acquainted with the blog and their focus. Do not send out a blind pitch.
   - [ ] Make your pitch personalized to show you have done your research. Use actual names and any other references that might give you a competitive edge.
   - [ ] Spend time crafting the perfect subject line for your email pitch. "Blog pitch" isn't going to be enough to get an editor's attention. Be more proactive with something like "Nine reasons authors need to use Pinterest."
   - [ ] Include:
     - [ ] Intro to who you are (with any credentials).
     - [ ] What value do you bring to their audience?
     - [ ] Share multiple article ideas.

- ☐ Outline perceived takeaway for the audience.
- ☐ Great royalty/license-free visuals.
  - TIP: Pitch **ideas** not the final draft.
- ☐ Follow the guidelines:
  - ☐ tone
  - ☐ formatting
  - ☐ topics
  - ☐ most popular
- ☐ Proofread your content. Prove that you have pride in your perfection.
- ☐ Follow up, but respect the process and give the editors time to review your pitch.

Blog	URL	Audience	Contact	Date/Ideas Pitched

- ☐ You're the bomb! Add this completed task to today's calendar!
- ☐ **Add to Calendar:** *Send out pitches whenever you have something viable to share.*

Social Media

"Social media creates communities, not markets"
Don Schultz

Marketing in general can be seen by many authors as a daunting part of the publishing business but social media, in particular, can seem a strange and overwhelming world to navigate. Finding the right platform to engage with your target market, however, can lead to increasing your visibility, cultivating an audience and increasing your discoverability. All of that ultimately leads to more books sales!

Building your social media presence starts with finding a channel that you (and your target market) are comfortable with. Each of the various platforms has its unique aspects, however the general rules of branding and marketing remain largely the same. As always, consistency is key.

Disclaimer*: All of these tasks are based on information provided by the platforms in January 2018. I have listed direct links to the individual platform tutorials which should remain up-to-date. Marketing suggestions may no longer be viable when platforms update, change or delete options. Such is social media…*

Reference: SOCIAL MEDIA OPTIONS

Category: Social Media

Where is your target market and how do you master the platform to reach them?

Platform	User #	Gender	Age	Interesting Fact
Facebook	2.1 billion	83% of online women, 75% of online men	18 - 49	75% of Facebook users spend at least 20 minutes on Facebook every day.
YouTube	1.5 billion	55% of online men, 45% of online women	18 - 49	Two million video views per minute
Instagram	800 million	38% of online women, 26% of online men	Under 35	53% of Instagram users follow brands
Twitter	330 million	22% of online men, 15% of online women	18 - 29	53% of Twitter users never post any updates
Pinterest	250 million	45% of online women, 17% of online men	18 - 64	Users referred by Pinterest are 10% more likely to make a purchase on e-commerce than users of other networks.
LinkedIn	106 million	31% of online men, 27% of online women	30 - 64	45% of people making $75K/year or more use LinkedIn

Task: FACEBOOK ANALYTICS
Category: Social Media

You need reliable data to measure the return on investment (ROI) of your marketing efforts. Free social media platforms make their money from advertising dollars, so they want you to be successful in advertising with them. To ensure that you have the best advantages to succeed, they provide you with analytical data.

Facebook calls its business page data *Insights* which is a powerful marketing tool to track fan engagement and page performance. It also gives you (the administrator of the page) the opportunity to gather demographic information about the followers of your page. Growing your page organically (and not stacking it with false like-for-like numbers or paid-for followers) will provide you the data to maximize your sharing strategy and further define your audience to get your marketing more laser focused. Reviewing the data allows you to see what works and what should not be repeated.
- From the horse's mouth: https://analytics.facebook.com/

Step-by-step:
1. Log into your Facebook page.
2. Click Insights at the top of the page.
3. The menu bar on the left side of the page will help you navigate the pages.

The Checklist:

- ☐ Overview: a digested version of your analytics.
  - TIP: Each section has an information icon in the top right corner to clarify definitions.
  - TIP: One of the most helpful options on the overview is the *Pages to Watch* section, which gives you the option of comparing your page data to other similar (competitive) pages. Consider adding the authors that you chose earlier (page 15). Make note of the number of times they post and what their engagement is like. For inspiration, visit their page to see how they are doing what they do, and give some of those techniques a try.

- ☐ Promotions: a closer look at how your paid advertising compares, so you can determine what your ROI (Return on Investment) is and what you should duplicate.

☐ Followers: the total number of followers (not likes) per day and where those likes happened.
- If a person follows your page, your Facebook page posts will appear on their personal Facebook feed.
- Followers have the option to *Unfollow* your page but still like your page. That means your content will not show up in their feed anymore.

☐ Likes: the total number of likes (not followers) per day and where those likes came from. Likes tend to be highly overrated.
- TIP: The default setting when someone likes your page means that they also follow your page, but they can opt out of following you at any time.

☐ Reach: post reach can be organic (cultivated by you) or it can be likes and follows that come from paid advertising on the platform.
- Reactions, Comments, Shares, and more also can be researched on this page.
- TIP: Engagement is key, so copy the posts that get the greater engagement.

☐ Page Views: who saw your page.
- The section they saw.
- Demographics of the viewers.
- Origin of viewers.

☐ Actions on Page: the number of actions users took on your page.
- This would include clicking directions, phone number or website links.
- There is also a chart with CTAs (Calls to Action) and the demographics of the people who clicked on the CTA button.

☐ Posts: analysis of your previous posts including the reach and engagements (post clicks or reactions/comments/shares).

☐ Events: reach and response to events from your events page.

☐ Videos: overview of videos (including slideshows) that appear on your page, as well as duration watched.

☐ Groups: data on any group associated with your page. For instance if you have a group for your street team and another for beta readers, that information would be found here. Note that individual groups also have *Insights* but this puts multiple groups on the same page for comparison.

☐ People: provides demographic information about the people who like your page (based on information from their Facebook user profiles). This is one of the most intriguing data breakdowns!
  • Information includes gender, age, country, city and language.
  • These statistics will be helpful in determining your actual audience

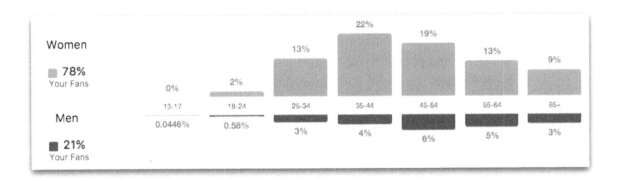

Notes: _____

_____

_____

_____

_____

_____

_____

☐ **You're on your way! Add this completed task to today's calendar!**
☐ **Add to Calendar:** *Get in the habit of checking your Facebook analytics at least every other week, more often if your author page is busy. Once you determine the frequency that works for you, add to the calendar.*

Task: SOCIAL MEDIA HEADERS
Category: Social Media

Headers are what people see first when they visit your space on any of the social media platforms. They are much like the cover of your book: they make the first impression and hopefully entice viewers to poke around to find out more.

The Checklist:
1. Things to remember no matter what the platform:
   - ☐ Size matters: each platform has its own dimensions and guidelines, and what works for one platform may distort in another.
   - ☐ Sizes change: use a tool with up-to-date, pre-sized templates
     - Canva has an option to resize headers for different platforms without starting over each time. The upgrade to Canva for Work is $12.95 per month (slightly less if you pay for the year).
     - Bannersnack is another tool that resizes headers across different platforms. It has a limited-access free trial with single user upgrades from $7 to $18 a month.
   - ☐ Branding: use the things you determined in your author-branding tasks and strive for cohesion across platforms.
   - ☐ Make headers visually interesting: not just a sales pitch.
   - ☐ Less is more; don't let your headers become a jumbled mess.
   - ☐ Variety: headers don't need to be changed every day, but change is a good way to avoid stagnation.
   - ☐ Plan ahead; use your calendars to sort out themes for your headers, and design them in advance.

2. Tips for social media headers:
   - ☐ Facebook headers can now be videos instead of just static images on business pages.
     - ☐ Create the video so that it makes sense without sound in case the viewer has the sound off.
     - ☐ Video length should be between 20 and 90 seconds
     - ☐ Recommended size is 820 x462 pixels.
   - ☐ Promote a call to action (CTA). For example:
     - ☐ Buy my book!
     - ☐ Visit my website.
     - ☐ Sign up for our free marketing videos.

- [ ] Should duplicate the CTA button options.
- [ ] Branding!
    - [ ] Be mindful of colors, elements, tagline, and logo.
    - [ ] Maintain your voice.
- [ ] Point out a problem that your book solves. For example:
    - [ ] "Hungry?" with a picture of your cookbook.
    - [ ] "36% of Americans have traveled outside the US. This book is for the other 64%," for your travel book.
- [ ] Focus on fan involvement. For example:
    - [ ] Show pictures from a recent photo contest of readers with your books.
    - [ ] Use fan art.
- [ ] Blow your own horn with a new award, accolade, or milestone announcement.
- [ ] Occasionally, just sell your product.
- [ ] Promote an upcoming event.
- [ ] Create buzz for a work-in-progress.

    TIP: Use Canva to create dynamic social media headers.

3. Brainstorm on ideas for your headers. Change them up at least monthly.

_____

_____

_____

_____

_____

_____

_____

- [ ] **Brilliantly done! Add this completed task to today's calendar!**
- [ ] **Add to Calendar:** *Change your header at least once a month.*

Task: FACEBOOK LIVE VIDEO

Category: Social Media

You have probably seen a Facebook Live video by now. They are popular with everyone who wants to share a sunset or who is sharing breaking news or a social injustice. What you might not understand yet is how to leverage this Facebook feature to promote your author page, build your brand, and increase your reach.

Facts:

- Live videos created in Facebook will be saved to your timeline so viewers can watch it at any time, even if they miss it when it's actually live. It also means you can use the video for a variety of other purposes: a blog post, an episode on your YouTube channel, a Patreon page, Kickstarter campaign, or newsletter.

- Notifications are sent to all of the people that like your page, not just those who interact with it, which greatly increases your reach.

- In its ranking algorithm, Facebook prioritizes live feeds over other video options.

- You can now create a Facebook Live video within groups that you are a member of as well.

Step-by-Step:

1. Go to your author page on Facebook (either through Facebook or Page Manager)
2. Go to Write something… as if you were going to write a new post.
3. Select the video icon next to *Go Live*.
   TIP: There are a lot of fun masks that you can use, but keep in mind that this is to promote your book or your author brand, so be professional.
4. Click Start Live Video and make your video.
5. When you are finished, click Done. Voila! You have just completed a Facebook Live video!

The Checklist:

- Before the video:
  ☐ Tools needed: a steady desktop tripod (there are many options for under $15), cell phone with a decent camera, and an external microphone (optional but will increase the sound quality in most cases — price ranges between $15-$50)
  ☐ Ideal length for most Facebook Live videos is less than 18 minutes.

☐ Start with a compelling title and keep it targeted to your audience.

- During the video:
  ☐ Go live. Start strong with your hook in the first 10 seconds.
    - TIP: Don't wait for viewers to start watching before you get to the message. Most of your audience will see the video in the rebroadcast, not actually "live." Don't make your audience wait around.
  ☐ Have valuable content ready. It is okay to use notes to stay on track. Your audience will appreciate your efforts. Their time is important.
  ☐ Establish yourself as an authority to new viewers, but be brief. They don't need your life story, just a reason to be listening to you. Your name and a one sentence bio related to the topic will suffice.
  ☐ Interact with the audience but not to distraction.
    - TIP: Verbal calls-to-action (CTAs) add to engagement, such as "Who loves this idea? Press the heart button to let me know," or "Turn on notifications if you don't want to miss my next video."
    - TIP: Add calls-to-comment (CTCs) to increase interaction, such as "Tag someone in the comments who needs to watch this video," or "I'm interested in what sorts of books you read. Leave me a comment telling me." Don't forget to interact with the commenters after the video is done.
  ☐ Q&A is always good for interaction but if you don't have many/any viewers (think of the rebroadcast) suggest that viewers leave any questions in the comment section. You can either address them in a future video or respond to them in the comments.
    - TIP: Pay attention to the questions asked, as it may let you know about points that were confusing or omitted from your original video. Adjust in the future.

- After the video:
  ☐ You can edit the title, choose a different thumbnail, or upload a custom one.
  ☐ You can add a caption (captions give your video a 14% increase in engagement).
  ☐ Engage with rebroadcast viewers.
  ☐ Use the video in your Facebook ads!
  ☐ Upload the video for use on Twitter, Instagram, and YouTube.

☐ **Three cheers for you! Add this completed task to today's calendar!**
☐ **Add to Calendar:** *Consider a weekly video for consistency.*

Task: SCHEDULE FACEBOOK POSTS

Category: General Marketing

Years ago, a business needed to have a Yellow Pages ad to be competitive and to be found by consumers. By the early 90s, it became obvious that businesses would need to create websites on the internet in order to compete in the marketplace.

Today there are over 60 million businesses that have a business Facebook page. Social media has created unique ways for businesses to be able to interact with their customer base in real time. In fact, according to statistics, 42% of customer service responses happen during the first 60 minutes.

The downside, of course, is that creating content takes a lot of time and effort on the part of the business. As an authorpreneur, you are most often running a one-person enterprise, and time is a precious commodity. One of the biggest timesavers is scheduling social media content in advance. For the sake of this task, we will cover how to schedule Facebook posts specifically. We will offer other options for multi-platform scheduling in another task.

Note: This feature is only available for your business (author) page. At this time, personal accounts cannot preschedule posts.

How-to Steps:
1. Create your post as you normally would. Note: you can use photos, videos, or tags just like you always do.
2. Select Publish and you will see a pull-down menu. Select Schedule.

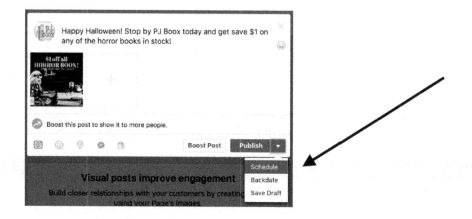

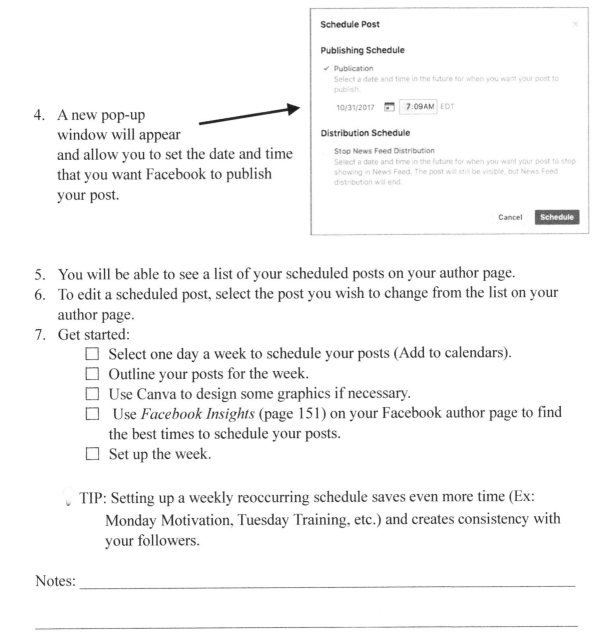

4. A new pop-up window will appear and allow you to set the date and time that you want Facebook to publish your post.

5. You will be able to see a list of your scheduled posts on your author page.
6. To edit a scheduled post, select the post you wish to change from the list on your author page.
7. Get started:
    - ☐ Select one day a week to schedule your posts (Add to calendars).
    - ☐ Outline your posts for the week.
    - ☐ Use Canva to design some graphics if necessary.
    - ☐ Use *Facebook Insights* (page 151) on your Facebook author page to find the best times to schedule your posts.
    - ☐ Set up the week.

    TIP: Setting up a weekly reoccurring schedule saves even more time (Ex: Monday Motivation, Tuesday Training, etc.) and creates consistency with your followers.

Notes: _____

_____

_____

_____

☐ **What a superstar! Add this completed task to today's calendar!**
☐ **Added to Calendar:** *pick a consistent day of the week that you can preschedule a week's worth of posts* **x52.**

Task: SCHEDULE SOCIAL POSTS

Category: Social Media

Manually posting, especially to multiple platforms, can be stressful and time-consuming. Less time posting and coming up with content on the fly means more time for interaction with your readers. Scheduling your social media posts ahead also leads to consistency, which leads to better branded posts, which leads to better engagement. It's a win all the way around!

See also page 158 for Facebook scheduling details.

Checklist:

☐ The chart below offers a generic outlook of best post times on the five most popular platforms.

Platform	Mon	Tues	Wed	Thu	Fri	Sat	Sun
Facebook			3pm	1-4pm	1-4pm	12-1pm	12-1pm
Twitter	12-3pm	12-3pm	noon 5-6pm	12-3pm	12-3pm	12-3pm	
Instagram	not 3-4pm			not 3-4pm			
Pinterest	2-4am 2-4pm	2-4am 2-4pm	2-4am 2-4pm	2-4am 2-4pm	3pm	2-4am	8-11 am
YouTube	9pm-8am	9pm-8am	9pm-8am	9pm-8am	9pm-8am	9pm-8am	

☐ If your audience is in different time zones, you can schedule your content for times that you may not even be available.

☐ You want to make sure that you are posting often enough to be seen, but not too much to be annoying. So how often should you post each day on each platform?
- Facebook: no more than 2x per day
- Twitter: 3x per day (or more)
- Instagram: 1.5 times per day (or more)
- Pinterest: 5 times a day (or more)
- YouTube: 1x per day

☐ Watch your analytics for each platform to monitor what types of ads and what times are getting the best interaction.

☐ If you are on only one platform, you might be better off just setting up a schedule and just working within their system.
  ☐ TWITTER tutorial: https://business.twitter.com/en/help/campaign-editing-and-optimization/scheduled-tweets.html
  ☐ YOUTUBE tutorial: https://support.google.com/youtube/answer/1270709?hl=en

☐ Pinterest and Instagram need 3rd party applications to schedule posts in advance. Be sure to find the right scheduler for your platforms. Some of the more popular scheduling platforms to check out are:
  ☐ Hootsuite
  ☐ Buffer
  ☐ Post Planner
  ☐ Sprout Social

Notes: _____

_____

_____

_____

_____

_____

_____

_____

☐ **Props to you! Add this completed task to today's calendar!**
☐ **Add to Calendar:** *Once a week!*

	SUN	MON	TUES	WED	THU	FRI	SAT

SOCIAL MEDIA POSTING SCHEDULE

Task: PAID SOCIAL ADVERTISING

Category: General Marketing

Paid social media advertising is often a confusing and changing challenge for many small business owners, indie authors included. Many people will tell you that Facebook or Instagram advertising doesn't work, and, in fairness, it probably didn't work for them. More than likely, it was really a matter of not fully understanding the way marketing works in general.

There isn't enough room in this book to go into the nuances and strategies of each individual social platform's advertising algorithms. Instead, I will give you a few tips on some marketing basics and tell you where you can find the information to help you better navigate the waters of paid social advertising.

The Checklist:

• FACEBOOK: https://www.facebook.com/business/learn/facebook-tips-recommendations

- ☐ Use the information from your Facebook *Insights* (page 151) to help you identify your audience and their habits.
- ☐ Create unique ad sets for different audiences (An ad set is a group of ads that share the same daily or lifetime budget, schedule, bid type, bid info, and targeting data).
- ☐ Send your audience to specific destinations (not www.yourwebsite.com but rather www.yourwebsite.com/facebookad1).
- ☐ Facebook will refuse an ad that has more than 40% text so be sure to choose an attention-getting image. Make sure that you pay attention to any licensing needed.
- ☐ Watch your budget. Pay attention to what your daily or total spending is. Research any terms you don't fully understand.

• Other platforms with advertising tutorials:
- ☐ TWITTER: https://business.twitter.com/en/twitter-ads.html
- ☐ INSTAGRAM: https://business.instagram.com/advertising
- ☐ PINTEREST: https://ads.pinterest.com/
- ☐ YOUTUBE: https://www.youtube.com/yt/advertise/

☐ **Crack open the bubbly! Add this completed task to today's calendar!**
- ☐ **Add to Calendar:** *Add social media advertising to your marketing plan as your budget allows.*

Calendars

**"We are what we repeatedly do.
Excellence, then, is not an act, but a habit."**
Will Durant

The calendar pages were created blank so that you can start at any year, month, or day and work daily for the next twelve months.

Check the calendar before you begin a task each day to see if a recurring or follow-up task is already scheduled. Complete details on how to manage the calendars can be found in the **First Things First** section on page 14.

If you write down the tasks as you complete them, in addition to scheduling upcoming tasks, you will be creating a blueprint of your marketing strategies for a year. The information that you have gathered to complete the task will become a resource that you can revisit as you plan the next year of marketing your indie books!

MONTH #1 _____

Other stuff to remember:

_____

_____

_____

_____

_____

_____

_____

_____

_____

_____

_____

_____

MONTH #2 _____

Other stuff to remember:

_____

_____

_____

_____

_____

_____

_____

_____

_____

_____

_____

_____

_____

MONTH #3 _____

Other stuff to remember:

_____

_____

_____

_____

_____

_____

_____

_____

_____

_____

_____

_____

_____

MONTH #4 _____

Other stuff to remember:

_____

_____

_____

_____

_____

_____

_____

_____

_____

_____

_____

_____

_____

MONTH #5 _____

Other stuff to remember:

_____

_____

_____

_____

_____

_____

_____

_____

_____

_____

_____

_____

MONTH #6 _____

Other stuff to remember:

_____

_____

_____

_____

_____

_____

_____

_____

_____

_____

_____

_____

_____

MONTH #7 _____

Other stuff to remember:

MONTH #8 _____

Other stuff to remember:

_____

_____

_____

_____

_____

_____

_____

_____

_____

_____

_____

_____

_____

MONTH #9 _____

Other stuff to remember:

_____

_____

_____

_____

_____

_____

_____

_____

_____

_____

_____

_____

Other stuff to remember:

_____

_____

_____

_____

_____

_____

_____

_____

_____

_____

_____

_____

_____

MONTH #11 _____

Other stuff to remember:

_____

_____

_____

_____

_____

_____

_____

_____

_____

_____

_____

_____

_____

MONTH #12 _____

Other stuff to remember:

_____

_____

_____

_____

_____

_____

_____

_____

_____

_____

_____

_____

**If you found value in this book,
please leave a review on one of the following websites:**

Amazon:
www.amazon.com/author/pbj

Goodreads:
www.goodreads.com/pbjauthor

PJ Boox:
www.pjboox.com/author/pbj

Barnes & Noble:
www.bn.com

…and tell your friends!

**Interested in bulk / wholesale purchases
for your group or workshop?**
Contact: publisher@pjinxpress.com

Follow Author Patti Jefferson:
Facebook: www.facebook.com/pbjauthor
Twitter: @pbjauthor

Follow PJ Boox Bookstore on:
Facebook: www.facebook.com/pjboox
Twitter: @pjboox
Instagram: @pjboox

PJ's Resource Guide

This is a list of some of my go-to resources. I have had good experiences with all of them so I feel comfortable in sharing them with you.

Full disclosure: In some instances, I do have an affiliate link for a particular company, but I would recommend them even if I didn't.

Author Organizations:
Alliance of Independent Authors @ *www.pjboox.net/alli*
Florida Authors and Publishers @ *www.myfapa.org*

Marketing Material Resources
PressGeek @ *www.pressgeek.com*
VistaPrint @ *www.vistaprint.com*
QR Code @ *www.qr-code-generator.com*

Marketing Books
Jab, Jab, Jab, Right Hook by Gary Vaynerchuk @ *www.garyvaynerchuk.com/books*
Weird & Wacky Holiday Marketing Guide by Ginger Marks @ *wwww.gingermarksbooks.com*

SWAG
Garrett Specialties @ www.garrettspecialties.com
Sticker Mule @ www.stickermule.com

Free Music for Videos
Kevin McLeod @ *incompetech.com*

School Visits
Kim Norman's FREE on-line resources @ *www.coolschoolvisits.com*
Schools: A Niche Market for Authors by Jane R. Wood @ *www.janewoodbooks.com*

About the Author:
Patti Brassard Jefferson

Author, Illustrator, Public Speaker, Bookstore Owner, Publisher

www.pbjauthor.com

Born in upstate New York in the early 60's, Patti Brassard was an early bookworm, notebook scribbler, and creator of random art projects. Not much changed when the family relocated to Virginia when she was in sixth grade. Art class was her happy place and english was her favorite subject.

Not exactly suited for a job around normal people, Jefferson ran her own graphic design business, a paint-it-yourself pottery studio, and finally an art gallery when she chased the sun to Florida in 2010.

In 2013, Jefferson finally released her first children's book, **How Long Will You Love Me** through Halo Publishing International. She followed that up with **Stu's Big Party** in 2014 which went on to win a FAPA Silver Medal. With two illustrated books under her belt, she started to illustrate picture books for other authors including the award-winning books: **You're a Crocagator** by Kenny Rager (2015) and **Bode the Beach Dog: Life is Ruff** (2016) by Tara and Geoff Moser.

While trying to get her books into retail locations, Jefferson became frustrated with the options and, after much research, opened the Gulf Coast Bookstore - one of the very first all indie author bookstores in the world. Six months later, in October of 2015, she opened the first P.J. Boox.

When not writing, illustrating, or running the bookstore, Jefferson likes to create large scale mosaics or repurpose discarded, curb-shopped furniture.

Her very favorite things to do are: reading picture books with her favorite little Blueberry, drinking wine and watching Sex and the City reruns with her brilliant daughter, and spending time near the water with her IslandBoy and two rescued mutts. Throw in a tiara, some sidewalk chalk and a funky reggae beat and you will see pure joy.

Clearly, she has learned to embrace her creative weirdness.

Special thanks to:

- Tara Alemany, *founding partner, Emerald Lake Books and multi-award-winning author of The Plan that Launched a Thousand Books*

- Greg Scott, *IT professional and author of Bullseye Breech*

- Richelle Renae, *author of a group of short stories in the educational Read Write Ponder series.*

Huge thanks to my tribe:

- *Lisa*, who challenged me to either be someone who wrote a book once or start a career as an author/illustrator/speaker. I blame her for a lot of this.

- *Mark*, who wrote me a nice email once and let me stalk him until I was comfortable in my own skin.

- *Tim*, who didn't have the heart to tell me I was nuts and went along for the ride.

- Linda, Faith, Lona, Julie, Marjorie, Judy, PK, Scott, and the rest of the Creative Weirdos for… well… being weird.

- *The Board of Directors of Florida Authors and Publishers (past and present),* who oddly lets me be a part of some pretty cool stuff.

- *Jenn*, my favorite brainstorming partner.

- *Amber*, the hippie chick, who loves glitter and also more glitter.

- *Rob*, the new guy, who finally came over to the dark side.

- *Jules*, who is one of my favorite #girlswithoptions.

- *My mom,* who showed me how to get through life with a "how hard can it be" attitude toward trying new things. If I truly am a disrupter, that's probably all her doing.

- *My dad*, who is taught me how to tell time (which I widely ignore), change my own tire (yay, me!) and stand up for myself.

- *Nikki*, who is kind and brilliant and organized and a talented writer in her own right. One of those things she did NOT get from me.

- And of course, *my IslandBoy,* who doesn't always understand why I do what I do but, apparently, is entertained enough to stick around anyway.

About P.J. Boox Bookstore

A Different Sort of Bookstore

In April of 2015, Patti Brassard Jefferson opened the Gulf Coast Bookstore in Fort Myers, FL with a partner. It originally featured only 36 local authors. Publishers Weekly called it "The First Bookstore Dedicated to Self-Published Authors."

Six months later, she opened the first PJ Boox bookstore. To date, hundreds of authors from all over the world have been featured there. Currently, almost 300 authors in dozens of genres are available in the Fort Myers location.

If you are an author with professionally produced books looking to get your book on the shelves of PJ Boox, please visit www.pjboox.net for author information and submission guidelines.

Retail site: www.pjboox.com
Phone: 239-437-3227

About P.J. Inx Press

Indie Publishing for Creative Weirdos

PJ Inx Press was launched in 2017 with the release of *365 Bright Ideas for Marketing Your Indie Books*. Our mission is to create educational content for niche markets and to provide opportunities that exemplify the spirit, creativity and collaborative nature of independent creators.

If you have a creative project that you'd like for PJ Inx Press to consider, please send a query to publisher@pjinxpress.com.

Upcoming projects include:
    #GirlsWithOptions
    Anthologies for Indies

Made in the USA
Las Vegas, NV
14 August 2021